PRISONER OF THE RISING SUN

PRISONER OF
THE RISING SUN

Stanley Wort

ISIS
LARGE PRINT
Oxford

Copyright © Stanley Wort, 2009

First published in Great Britain 2009
by
Pen & Sword Military
An imprint of Pen & Sword Books Ltd.

Published in Large Print 2010 by ISIS Publishing Ltd.,
7 Centremead, Osney Mead, Oxford OX2 0ES
by arrangement with
Pen & Sword Ltd.

British Library Cataloguing in Publication Data
Wort, Stanley.
    Prisoner of the rising sun. - - (Reminiscence)
    1. Wort, Stanley.
    2. Great Britain. Royal Navy- -History- -World War,
    1939–1945.
    3. World War, 1939–1945- -Prisoners and prisons,
    Japanese.
    4. Prisoners of war- -Great Britain.
    5. Prisoners of war- -Japan.
    6. Prisoners of war- -China- -Hong Kong.
    7. World War, 1939–1945- -Personal narratives,
    British.
    8. Large type books.
    I. Title II. Series
    940.5'472'52'092–dc22

ISBN 978–0–7531–9550–5 (hb)
ISBN 978–0–7531–9551–2 (pb)

Printed and bound in Great Britain by
T. J. International Ltd., Padstow, Cornwall

Contents

Contents

Maps

Preface

When the Second World War broke out in September 1939 I was two months short of my nineteenth birthday and living in England. Conscription had been introduced just before the war began and the first conscripts were called up in August 1939. People were called up according to their age group and the first to go were the 21-year-old young men. I was swept up in the patriotic fever that gripped the country when the war started and wanted to do my bit. I tried to join the Royal Air Force but in the period termed the "phoney war" the RAF was not accepting recruits. So when in February 1940 three colleagues, all of whom had nautical connections and nautical experience, decided to go to the Royal Navy recruiting office in Reading to join the Navy, I was persuaded to go with them even though I knew nothing of the sea. They argued that it would be far better for us to go and join up now and join the Navy than wait to be called up and have to go into the Army, where if the war followed the pattern of the First World War we would probably end up fighting in the trenches. For reasons I never discovered the other three were rejected and only I was accepted as an "Ordinary Signalman for the duration of hostilities".

I was sent to HMS *Royal Arthur* for three months' training. HMS *Royal Arthur* was a naval shore establishment on the east coast near the town of

Skegness. Prior to the war it had been a popular holiday camp and we recruits were housed in the chalets which previously had been occupied by holidaymakers. We were taught how to march, how to row, how to salute, how to sling a hammock and how to lash it up. On the way we also learned semaphore and the Morse code. We practised the latter with an Aldis signal lamp but at the end of our training even the best of us only managed to read one letter at a time, and then only if the signal was made very slowly. Nevertheless at the end of our three months we were all passed out as Ordinary Signalmen with a badge to prove it.

The narrative that follows describes what befell me between leaving the training camp and leaving the Royal Navy some six years later. I have also written briefly about the post-war years on matters that might interest the reader. As regards the prisoner-of-war years I have not attempted to include a detailed chronological account of my experiences. Over sixty years have passed since I was incarcerated and even though I have some notes written whilst a POW, it is impossible to recall every detail of what happened between December 1941 and August 1945. Furthermore I do not have the skill to convey in words the apprehension, the hunger, the frustration and often the pain and the fear that permeated the prison camps. Accordingly, I have restricted this account to events and experiences that are indelibly etched in my mind and might be of sufficient interest to be worth committing to print. A strong element of chance is manifest in many of them but whether this is random or preordained — "karma" as the Japanese would call it — the reader must decide for himself.

This work is dedicated to the memory of those members of the Hong Kong garrison in December 1941 who did not make it home, and especially to my very good friends Yeomen of Signals Bud Fisher and Peewee Symonds.

Stanley Wort

Acknowledgements

In producing this narrative I have received invaluable assistance and encouragement from two other Second World War Royal Navy veterans: Arthur Ray, who as a Fleet Air Arm pilot flew Swordfish aircraft in the Atlantic and Norwegian theatres, and Grumman Avengers in the Pacific; and Bill Fullilove, who spent his war in landing craft, and in one such vessel landed American troops on Omaha Beach on D-Day, 6 June 1944. My grateful thanks to both of them.

Stanley D. Wort

CHAPTER
ONE

On the Road to Cathay

That I came to be in Hong Kong in December 1940 is the direct result of having a surname the first letter of which is at the end of the alphabet. When in July 1940, after three months' instruction, my class passed out of the naval training school as Ordinary Signalmen (Hostilities Only), we were told that we were to be divided into four groups, which were to be allocated to four naval bases: Chatham, Portsmouth, Plymouth and Lowestoft; allocation would be made by drawing first a location and then a name from hats held by our two petty officer instructors. When the allocation was finished we would be given thirty minutes during which anybody could exchange allocation if he found someone willing to change with him. At the end of the half hour all allocations became final and we were stuck with whatever port name we held in our hand.

I drew Lowestoft, which before the war had been a very active fishing port but now housed a variety of small craft, in particular minesweepers and coastal steamers. As soon as the draw was completed a classmate came up to me and asked if I would swap with him. He was married with two small children and

1

lived in Lowestoft, but had drawn Portsmouth. As it happened that was near where my parents were living at the time so without thinking I agreed. As a result a few days later I was sent with fourteen classmates to Portsmouth barracks. Because of our limited ability as signalmen we were told at the training camp that we were destined for minesweepers and other small craft in the North Sea and elsewhere. But Portsmouth had different ideas for within a week of arrival in the grossly overcrowded pre-Victorian age barracks we were sent on thirty-six hours embarkation leave and told that on our return we would be sent to the battleship HMS *Warspite* in the Mediterranean, "for dispersal". I did not foresee at the time that it would be the only leave I would have during my six years in the Navy — and even that was spoiled by enemy action. I went home to Southampton and my father, my sister and I took a tram down to the town pier, a favorite haunt of ours. We had no sooner arrived there than the air-raid sirens began their mournful wail and we had to dive into an air-raid shelter. We heard two explosions before the "all clear" was sounded about a half hour after we had entered the shelter. When we emerged we saw that a pub some hundred yards away had been hit, and air-raid wardens and firemen were searching for casualties. A policeman told us that it had been a hit-and-run raid by a few Stuka dive-bombers. We returned home and I left at five o'clock the next morning in order to catch the train back to Portsmouth. Despite the early hour, as always, my mother was there to see me off.

I was glad to be getting out of the barracks where we had to live out of our kitbags (which we had to keep locked because theft was commonplace) and scramble every night to find a place to sling our hammocks. The barrack buildings were so antiquated that I am sure Nelson would have been familiar with them — the only concession to modernity since his day was the introduction of the electric light. When we returned from leave at seven o'clock that Sunday morning, we just hung around the barracks until noon before being sent to the mess hall for a midday meal having been told we would not be moving that day. Just as the meal finished, though, my name was called over the public address system telling me to report to the office of the Drafting Master at Arms. It took me quite a while to find where it was but when I finally got there I was told that because a regular signalman had failed to return from leave, and because mine was the last name alphabetically on the list of new boys, I was being sent in his place on a draft to "HMS *Sultan II*".

When in my innocence I inquired of the Drafting Master at Arms where or what Sultan II was, I was told in no uncertain terms not to ask silly ******* questions but to have my bag and hammock over at the heavy gun battery by 1700 hours. Not wishing to incur the Master's displeasure I said goodbye to my companions and did as I was told. At the heavy gun battery I joined ten other ratings and a petty officer, and discovered that Sultan II was the name of the Naval Base at Singapore. We went by train to London to overnight at the Union Jack Club and the next morning a bus took us to King's Cross Station where we boarded the boat train which took us to Liverpool Docks. There we embarked on the RMS *Strathmore* (a passenger liner belonging, I believe, to the Peninsular and Orient Line) as steerage-class passengers. We found ten other ratings already aboard, one of whom I was glad to see had been with me at the training school in Skegness. It soon became apparent that the ship was bound for Australia and that she was full of old people and two complete junior schools being evacuated down under. The ship sailed shortly after we boarded and moved out on a dull rainy August day into Liverpool Bay, and on to a very stormy, dark Irish Sea. The storm intensified as we sailed around Northern Ireland and worsened as we headed out into the Atlantic. It lasted four days and this being my first seagoing experience I was as sick as a dog. On the fifth day a boat drill was called and I had to rise from my sick bed (my bunk, in fact) and make my way up five flights of what I still called stairs but which I now know were ladders to the boat deck. There I leaned back against what I thought was the wall but was of course the bulkhead, and hoped to die, I felt so terrible. We were kept waiting by "our" lifeboat for nearly half an hour, we being thirty-eight old people and two naval ratings, one of whom had never been to sea before. When at last an officer came round and explained that by allocating two naval types to each lifeboat, experienced seamen would be available in all the lifeboats, I could hardly refrain from laughing, despite my nausea. Worse was to come, however, for as we were dismissed and I turned away to go down below and continue the dying process, an old lady touched my collar for luck and said, "You know, son, I have crossed the Atlantic twenty-two times and I have never known such a storm as the one we have just passed through. But I was not afraid — it makes us feel so safe to have you sailors on board." I could not think of a suitable comment so I mumbled "Thank you" and crawled away. It took me a long while to live down that incident.

The weather cleared on the sixth day out and so did my seasickness. I quite enjoyed the rest of the trip. The Strathmore was a ship of some 22,000 tons and because she was capable of cruising at 22 knots was designated an independently routed merchant vessel. This meant that she was fast enough to have a sporting chance of eluding submarines and therefore could proceed on her own as distinct from being part of a convoy, the speed of which is dictated by the slowest ship in it. We zigzagged all the way down the Atlantic and at dawn on the twenty-first day at sea, whilst I was on lookout duty, Table Mountain rose from the eastern horizon. It was a magnificent sight and as we approached the Cape and entered Cape Town harbour I thought what an attractive place this southern tip of Africa appeared to be. We were allowed ashore and the town lived up to my first impression. Having come from a land of blackouts and air raids, to me this brilliantly lit and ration-free city had something of a magical quality. Before the Strathmore sailed, four of our group were put ashore to await transport to the Simonstown naval base located to the east of Cape

Town. The next port of call was Mombasa in Kenya, where shore leave was granted once again and I had my first experience of tropical heat in an African city. I did not like it very much, nor did I care for Mombasa having, I suppose, been spoilt by the charm of Cape Town. By comparison Mombasa seemed an impoverished place with little to commend it except that it did have restaurants in one of which some friends and I ordered roast chicken, something none of us had seen for ages at home. When it came after a very long wait, even that was disappointing for we each received a whole chicken about the size of a small pigeon. It was only when we left the restaurant that we discovered why we had had to wait so long for our meal to be served. Round the side of the building we saw two of the waiters with choppers in their hands chasing an uncooperative flock of the smallest white chickens we had ever seen. We had obviously partaken of some very fresh food.

From Mombasa the *Strathmore* headed across the Indian Ocean to Bombay. The day before land was reached the skies darkened with what the experienced travellers said were monsoon rains. It was hot and oppressive; even the sea looked like molten lead and the smells of the city wafted out to the ship. We docked quite close to the "Gateway to India" monument and I remembered my father, a motor mechanic serving in the Army Service Corps, saying that he had seen it when he landed in Bombay twenty-five years earlier during the First World War. It made me think of him and his wartime experiences, and although I did not know it then, mine were to be very different. He went

6

north from Bombay to serve for three years on what was then called the North-West Frontier. Then in 1919, during the Afghan War, he nursed the first-ever motorized convoy through the Khyber Pass. It comprised some forty-two American Liberty trucks which had solid tyres, crash gearboxes and side-valve engines which overheated badly at the higher altitudes.[1]

The *Strathmore* remained in port for two days and I went ashore twice. I found Bombay a smelly, noisy place but it was very colourful and for the most part cheerful, although I was appalled at the number of beggars that abounded and the abject poverty that was apparent in some areas. One of the few things I remember about it was a servicemen's club to which a kindly English police officer had directed some of us. It was staffed by volunteers and all the serving ladies were Parsee. They were very white skinned, wore long saris, held themselves very upright and seemed to glide about the room. They had poise and style the like of which I had not seen before nor have ever seen since.

Before leaving Bombay for Colombo, two more of our little group were put ashore, so we arrived a few days later in the Sinalese capital with only fifteen left, four of whom were immediately put ashore for onward passage to the naval base at Trincamolee, on the island's north-east coast. Among those to go was my friend from the training school. The rest of us were again allowed ashore and my only recollections of Colombo are that it was a more attractive city than Bombay but that it was home to the world's craziest taxi drivers. We sailed after a very brief stay and headed for Singapore where I now knew that the naval base there was called Sultan II and my destination, or so I thought at the time.

When the ship arrived in Singapore the eleven remaining members of our party (ten ratings and one petty officer) were told to fall in on the boat deck with our bags and hammocks. This we duly did whereupon a lieutenant commander and a couple of chief petty officers came aboard and, after welcoming us to Singapore, told us to take one pace forward as our names were called. Ten names were called in alphabetical order, and then the instruction was given to "pick up your gear and proceed down the gangway." After the ten had done this, they were followed by the boarding party, leaving me all alone wondering what was going to happen next. I wondered for a long time because three hours passed before the Lieutenant Commander came aboard again but did not appear to be looking for me — in fact he walked right past me. I began to think that I had been abandoned or that as a result of some faulty communication I was not officially here so no one had any claim on me. In this frame of mind I made what a more experienced naval rating would consider a serious error of judgment — I sought out the officer and asked him what was to happen to me. Clearly what I should have done was lie low in the hope the ship would depart for Australia before the naval authorities in Singapore realized that they had another raw recruit on their hands. But in those days I was young and innocent. The officer looked at me with a friendly smile, pulled a list out of his pocket and having consulted it said, "Oh yes, you were last alphabetically on the list, you are not going to Sultan II but to HMS *Tamar*, the base ship in Hong Kong. I'll send a couple of chaps to help you get your gear over to the *Elenga*, the troopship that will take you to Hong Kong. I'm not sure when she will sail but you will be instructed by her skipper." True to his word a couple of hefty sailors arrived within half an hour, and helped me carry my bag and hammock to the *Elenga* which was docked about a quarter of a mile away. The *Elenga*, which had been built at the turn of the century, was an Indian troopship and her troop decks were filled with Indian soldiers bound for the China Station. I was allocated to an upper-deck cabin with the Indian officers with whom I spent a very pleasant week on the journey north. Before the *Elenga* left Singapore, though, I experienced an act of kindness which I remember to this day. The ship's captain was an Englishman, a real old-fashioned sea dog; when I was settled in he sent for me and told me that he did not know when he would be instructed to sail. He was confident, though, that he would get plenty of notice so I was free to go ashore as much as I liked, provided I reported back to him at noon each day to see whether sailing instructions had been received. He then asked if I had any money and when I said that I had about ten shillings he said, "That is not enough, take this — you may need it," and handed me a pound note. I was both grateful and embarrassed at the same time, but he brushed away my thanks. Even today I recall the

9

incident and am grateful for that stranger's act of kindness.

In the event I was unable to make use of my new-found wealth because the moment I stepped outside the dockyard gate dressed in my tropical white shorts I was arrested by the naval shore patrol! Apparently naval ratings on shore leave had to wear Number 6 uniforms (white tunic and bell bottoms trimmed with blue piping). I explained that as an "hostilities only" rating I had not been issued with a Number 6 suit, the closest thing to it that I possessed being an off-white calico "duck" suit (intended for use in combat so that wounds could be readily spotted. As the war progressed and set-piece, large-scale battles between opposing fleets became a thing of the past, the use of duck suits was dropped and none were issued to later recruits). After some discussion among the members of the shore patrol and a telephone call to naval HQ I was released and told I could come ashore if I changed into my duck suit. This I duly did but with temperatures in the 90s and humidity at 90 plus per cent, walking around in a heavy, course, calico duck suit was not very comfortable. There were few air-conditioned oasis in Singapore in those days open to the lower forms of animal life of which as an Ordinary Signalman I was a part, and so my exploration of Singapore was somewhat limited. On my return to the *Elenga* I was not sorry to learn that we were to sail the next day.

The old *Elenga* was transporting men of the Rajput and Punjabi regiments on her main decks with their officers housed in cabins on the upper deck, one of which I was allocated. She was no ocean greyhound and it took her a week to reach Hong Kong. As far as I was concerned, however, the longer the better for life on board was very pleasant. I had no duties to perform and I spent most of my time playing bridge with the Indian officers, some of whom were graduates of English universities; most of them spoke better English than I did. The diet in the mess, though, was very Indian — everything was curried including the breakfast bacon and eggs. I was somewhat apprehensive about my next move into the real regular Navy which I suspected would not suffer amateurs gladly. When we eventually docked in Kowloon my apprehension was justified for there, standing on the dock, was the largest, most formidable-looking Master at Arms I had ever seen. He was at least 6 foot 2 in height with a 44-inch waist and was dressed in immaculate whites. The gold of his cap badge glistened in the sun and a rainbow of medal ribbons adorned his massive chest, but it was the face that drew the attention. Carved out of the finest teak, the hooded eyes, the prominent nose and lantern jaw seemed the very essence of law and order, and the embodiment of all authority. He was accompanied by two members of the naval shore patrol. The latter came aboard and found me (the great man did not climb gangways to find junior ratings) and helped me down with my bag and hammock. Then they stood me to attention before "God". He looked down on me but said nothing — he did not have to for what is there for a professional sailor with decades of service to say to an amateur; if I could read anything in his eyes it was a look of pity. Abruptly, in a voice that came from deep within his huge frame, he snapped, "Get him aboard," the holiday cruise was over and I was back in the King's Navy!

Note:

1. Crash gearbox. In the early days of the motor car there were no automatic gearboxes, nor were there any synchro-mesh gears to facilitate a smooth manual gear change. Consequently when changing gear the driver had to try to match the speed of the drive cog in the gearbox drive chain with that of the one connected to the drive shaft. It was particularly difficult to do this when changing down and one had to learn the double declutch technique. This involved depressing the clutch and slipping the gear lever into neutral. You would then rev the engine and quickly depress the clutch and engage the lower gear. It still works well on modern cars equipped with synchromesh manual gearboxes, especially if the synchromesh cones are well worn.

CHAPTER TWO

On Life in the King's Navy

In the event my apprehension about life in the regular King's Navy proved to be groundless and the period from September 1940 until December 1941 turned out to be one of the happiest periods of my life. I was put aboard a naval pinnace which took me and the reception party from Kowloon across Hong Kong harbour to the Naval Dockyard in Victoria. On arrival we went aboard HMS *Tamar*, the Hong Kong base ship (she was an old wooden hulk which had once sailed the high seas under a combination of sail and steam power) where the Master at Arms handed me over to the tender mercies of the Senior Petty Officer Sick Berth Attendant in charge of the sick bay. There I was vaccinated and inoculated against every disease known to man (at least it felt that way but probably covered only smallpox, cholera, tetanus and yellow fever) and then subjected to a lecture and slide show about the dangers of venereal disease and the unpleasant things it can do to you. I survived that without fainting or vomiting but it was a close-run thing. When that was over I was taken to meet the man who presided over the department of which I had just

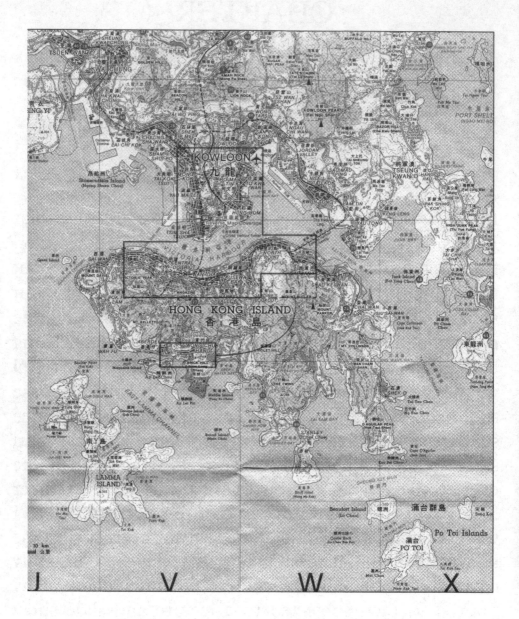

Hong Kong Island and Kowloon

become the most junior member — the Chief Yeoman of Signals.

He was a man whom I grew to admire, a fatherly figure who maintained discipline without ever raising his voice and whom I can now recognize as one of the best managers I have ever known. He welcomed me into his department, asked about what training I had had and whether I had ever been abroad before. As the answer to the former was very little by his standards (normal training time for a Royal Naval signalman in those days was five years) and to the latter, "No, I have never been outside England." He said, "Well, we will keep you here in the signal office to start with and continue your training for a while. For now you can go ashore every evening but for the first two weeks I will detail off a leading hand to accompany you. He will show you the way around, tell you the places that are out of bounds, explain the currency to you and have you back on board by eleven o'clock."

So began my life in the regular Navy. I was a bit of a curiosity to begin with because I was the first Hostilities Only rating seen in Hong Kong, and on my first Sunday there I caused a sensation at church parade. The whole ship's company was assembled on *Tamar*'s quarterdeck for a church service and dress of the day was No. 6 suits. Still without such a garment I was put in the back row in the hope, I suppose, that my duck suit would not be noticed. Unfortunately Rear Admiral Peters decided to do a full inspection row by row; when he got to me he stopped and all his following retinue came to a grinding halt behind him. He asked

15

me my name and how much training I had had, what conditions were like in Portsmouth Barracks and how much damage the air raids had done. I answered him as best I could and he went on talking to me for a few minutes, welcoming me to his command and saying the Navy very much appreciated the effort being been made by what he termed "our temporary staff". When the service finished people surrounded me from the Base Commander downward demanding to know what the Admiral had said to me. So I told them, including his statement that if I had any problems his door was always open. I think that rather surprised them as it had me and needless to say I never ventured near his office until I was summoned to attend there some fourteen months later.

Just as the regular Navy was curious about me I found some of its behaviour, to say the least, a little odd at first. For example, on my second day aboard Tamar I went for a shower. There were banks of showerheads situated in a spacious area on the lower deck of the forecastle. As there was no air-conditioning on board they were well used. When I arrived with my sponge bag and took out a piece of Lifebuoy Carbolic Soap which I had always used in England, an old (at least he seemed old to me at the time for he must have been at least forty) three-badge AB named Jackie Siddons shouted, "Don't use that stuff, it will take your skin off. Here, catch, borrow this."[1] What he threw me was a tablet of pink Camay toilet soap popular among ladies at home. For a while I wondered what kind of outfit I had joined. Two weeks later when I had my first

16

experience of "prickly heat" I realized that the old sailor's action was kindly meant and when I went ashore I bought myself some "glorious pink Camay".

Another thing that struck me as odd during my first days in Hong Kong was a peculiar happening on my first pay day (when I was handed the prodigious sum of ten Hong Kong dollars which had to last me for a month). I noticed that a number of sailors, Marines and some petty officers went over to a diminutive Marine bugler and handed him money. In some cases he appeared to hand some back. I subsequently learned that he was a moneylender whose terms were "nine for ten", or in the case of his more regular customers "ten for eleven". As the term for all loans ran from the day the money was borrowed until the end of the month in which it was borrowed (i.e. the next payday) it seemed to me that he was charging interest at about 120 per cent per annum. This was undoubtedly usury but nobody seemed to object even though he was known to visit the Hong Kong and Shanghai Bank frequently, in which it was rumoured he had substantial accounts.

It did not take long however for me to become accustomed to Navy life. I learned navalese and quickly understood that the "Andrew" meant the Navy and the ocean was referred to as "the ogie", "the jaunty" was the Master at Arms, "the Crusher" the Regulating Petty Officer, your "oppo" was your friend, "pigs" were the officers and all doctors were "quacks" (a term I am ashamed to admit I still use today). I was accepted as one of the troops and was subjected to innumerable "backward flashing exercises". It was during this initial period that I unknowingly gained a totally undeserved reputation for being a scribe. I had only been in Hong Kong for a couple of weeks when the Leading Hand of the mess asked me to write a letter for one of our number who was in trouble with the authorities. Apparently the signalman in question had not written home to his wife for six months and she had contacted the Naval Welfare people in England demanding to know what had happened to her husband. The matter eventually reached the Naval authorities in Hong Kong and the delinquent correspondent was summoned before the Commander. He was ordered to write a letter home within a week or spend the next two weeks in detention.

I asked the Leading Hand why our friend could not write his own letter and was told that he hardly knew how to write and found composing a letter very difficult. His oppo, who used to help him, had been posted back to the UK more than six months previously and our friend had not sent a letter home since then. So I asked how I was supposed to explain the lack of correspondence. "You are a bright, well-educated lad," the Leading Hand said. "Use your imagination." So I wrote something along the lines that my friend had broken his right arm playing football (he was a first-class centre forward) some months ago. Just as it was on the mend, but whilst his arm was still in a sling, he had been bitten on the thumb by some nasty insect of which we had plenty out there. The bite became septic and it took a long time to heal. That was why he had been unable to write and had asked me to write a letter for him. I explained how sorry he was not to have written and gave a carefully edited account of what he had been doing. I added the usual pleasantries and had him sign the letter with a cross. In a postscript I added that he hoped he would be able to write himself soon. In the event he did. Once every two or three weeks, until he too was posted back to the UK, I drafted a short letter for him and he would laboriously copy it out and send it. My reputation got around and whilst nobody wanted me to write a letter for them I was asked on half a dozen occasions for help in composing the most difficult of all letters to write. I remember one was to a sister, who after working a night shift in a factory went home to discover that her mother and her two baby daughters had been killed in an air raid. Another was to a mother to consol her on learning that the writer's two brothers had been killed in North Africa whilst serving in the Eighth Army. When I handed over suggested drafts I could see the depth of sorrow in the eyes of the person reading it. Tears were not far away in my eyes as well as theirs.

A few weeks after my arrival in the Colony I was posted to HMS *Scout*. On board this small, 900-ton, turtle-back destroyer it soon became obvious that although I was quite competent at semaphore I was never going to reach the required standard with the Aldis signal lamp to make me a worthwhile addition to the destroyer's signal staff. I could feel that I was more of a liability than an asset in the destroyer's crowded watchkeepers' mess, which comprised a steel box about 12 feet by 10. To enter one had to climb down a vertical ladder affixed to the bulkhead. At each side of the ladder were kit lockers and down the centre of the deck was a 10-foot-long table with benches each side. Around the other three sides were lockers about 2 feet high on top of which were long leather-covered cushions stuffed with horse hair. Normally there were fourteen members of the watchkeepers' mess — seven signalmen and seven telegraphists. When at sea and working in two watches there were never more than seven people in the mess at any one time, which meant there was just enough room for everybody to get their heads down — four on the cushioned lockers, one on the table and two on the two benches. When I came along as a supernumerary it caused a problem and sometimes I had to sleep under the table. Although I went on duty on the bridge with the rest of the watch I was never allowed to do anything — there was always a leading hand and at least one signalman wearing a Trained Operator badge to do any signalling that was called for. However, by happenstance, the *Scout*'s Yeoman did discover that I was pretty good at coding and decoding signals, so I spent most of my time on the destroyer doing just that and ensuring that the Captain's set of AFO's (Admiralty Fleet Orders) was kept up to date. (The codes used at that time were fairly straightforward numerical codes and as my mathematical ability was substantially better than my signalling skills, I found them easy to use.)

The three Hong Kong-based destroyers *Scout*, *Thanet* and *Thracian* that comprised the local naval defence force used to spend one week on patrol at sea, followed by one week as the "stand-by" vessel and then one week in reserve. Each time we went to sea I was seasick for the first day but then recovered — which was rather better than the Skipper who was sick most days and always had a bucket on the bridge. After I had been on the *Scout* for about eight weeks and we were in harbour as the stand-by vessel, the Port Signal Officer and the Chief Yeoman came aboard, and I noticed them talking to the ship's Yeoman and glancing at me. The next day I was transferred to the Central Signal Office. It happened at that time that the base signal office was desperately short of people to handle the mass of coded and ciphered communications that came in each night from the Admiralty in London.[2] It was therefore decided that I would be more usefully employed in the Signal Office than on a ship (and I do not think the *Scout*'s Yeoman was heartbroken to lose me) and I was allocated to one of the three watches that spent all their time receiving, sending, coding, decoding and disseminating information throughout the Naval Command, the Military Headquarters and Government House. When I first started everything was coded or decoded using naval numerical signal codes. Later, Codex and Cypher machines were introduced and I became quite adept at their use. As a result I was promoted to Signalman Trained Operator and my pay was increased by threepence a day! The coding job carried with it a number of "perks", not the least of which was the fact that one was permitted to live ashore on top of the Peak in Hong Kong. There the Admiralty owned two bungalows situated a quarter of a mile or so from the Peak tram upper terminus. One was occupied by the Naval C-in-C and the other allocated to the communications centre. It had been a recuperation ward attached to the Naval Hospital but as that establishment was almost empty now that the China Fleet had departed, it was opened to those doing watchkeeping duties at the centre. Residence there was voluntary and the majority of ratings preferred to stay aboard *Tamar* in order to avoid the half an hour travelling time before and after each watch. I thought that was a small price to pay for the amenities the bungalow had to offer. It provided plenty of space, there were hospital beds to sleep in and it was equipped with ceiling fans, all of which were sadly lacking aboard the base ship. Furthermore, the climate on the Peak was slightly more tolerable during the hottest months, when the humidity was at its worst, than in the dockyard. The location also meant that we escaped the crowded city and were able to endeavour to keep fit by jogging round Lugard Road that encircled Victoria Peak. From that road, or rather path, for it was not wide enough to accommodate vehicles, there were spectacular views over Lama Island, parts of Lantau Island and the city. At night, from that elevated vantage point, the city and Kowloon looked like a mass of sparkling jewels and as one of my friends described it, it was like standing on top of a Christmas tree and looking down on all the fairy lights.

Whilst stationed on the Peak I was surprised at some of the activities of regular naval personnel who lived there. One of the leading hands was an ardent lepidopterist. He had an enormous collection of butterflies and moths all mounted in glass-topped display cabinets especially made for him by Chinese cabinet-makers. Most of the collection had been caught in the viscinity of the Peak. The lush growth each side of the path that led down to the Dairy Farm facilities, not far from Aberdeen village, provided an ideal butterfly habitat. He showed me how to preserve and mount specimens and let me accompany him on some of his hunts for a particular variety. I recall that shortly before he was due to return to England he discovered that his specimen of the moon moth had been damaged. This particular moth, which had a wingspan of some 7 inches if I remember correctly, only came out as darkness approached. So with four amateur assistants he spent three evenings on the path to the Dairy Farm before one was caught and added to the collection. When he sailed for England the leading hand took the cabinets with him with the intention of presenting them to his home-town museum.

Another member of the Peak mess had become interested in religion. He had come across a group somewhere in the New Territories, which was endeavouring to merge the Christian faith with that of Islam and Judaism. I am not sure that I fully understood what was involved but it seemed to me that the group was aiming for the religious equivalent of Esperanto. Its basic argument being that all three religions worshipped the same god and that their only real difference was that they could not agree over who was his prophet. One day our religious friend drove me and a couple of other chaps out to the group's "monastery" (he was the only one among us that could drive and regularly hired a car to visit the place), past all the innumerable duck farms to a sight high on a hill overlooking the sea (probably Deep Bay). It was a modern building with the Cross, the Crescent and the Star of David mounted over its main entrance. The monks, if that is what they were, wore white robes or white trousers and jackets. Some were European, some Oriental and some looked to be Indian, although they may have been from the Middle East. They made us welcome and gave us tea, but no attempt was made to talk about religion. They seemed a pleasant lot and although their concept might be termed an oversimplification, it seemed to me that it had much to commend it. Together with a couple of other chaps, I went on another occasion with our religious-minded friend to visit the great golden statue of Buddha on Lantau Island. There was a ferry service from a dock on the central Victoria waterfront to Lantau Island which was the biggest offshore island in the Colony. From the landing jetty on the island a bus service took one up to the Buddhist Monastery with its giant statue, claimed to be the largest in the world. It was certainly impressive close to, built right on the top of a hill overlooking Hong Kong and the South China sea. We climbed up the long semi-circular flight of steps that lead to the base of the gold-clad Buddha and wondered how it had been built in such a precarious position. We went down the opposite semi-circular steps that lead us back to the monastery courtyard where there were stalls selling joss sticks, and what I suppose were prayer cards and other unrecognizable bits and pieces. You could enter part of the monastery and there, just inside the doors, were three or four more huge statues of what I presumed to be the Buddha, even though they were in glass cases and adorned in brightly coloured clothes. There was a strong smell of burning incense about the place and I was glad to get out of it, but I was pleased to have seen what to me at the time was an example of a very different world from mine.

By the time I was permitted to live on the Peak I had long since acquired two Number 6 suits and was no longer conspicuous ashore or at church parades. (These had been purchased with a kit allowance for the vast sum of HK$8.00 per made-to-measure suit from Mr Shan Tuck, tailor, of Wanchai). I began to explore the Colony in my time off, which to my surprise few of the regulars had bothered to do. Hong Kong was a fascinating city with vitality and an almost frenetic energy that made even London seem sluggish by comparison. It was also a very attractive city located at the foot of a steep hill up which ran the Peak tram. It operated on the same principal as the cliff lifts at some seaside resorts at home where the weight of the car descending helped pull up the ascending car. To a young man straight out from blacked-out England it was a fascinating place. Just walking down one of the main streets was an adventure. They were crowded with people in all sorts of costume. Street sellers hawked their wares, much of which were foodstuffs from which strange aromas filled the air. Large overcrowded trams clanged their way down the middle of the road, whilst cars, rickshaws and hand carts filled the remaining space. There were shops of every kind selling things I had never seen before and for the most part did not know what they were for. The one thing I particularly remember, for it appeared in the windows of most of the numerous restaurants both large and small, was a thing I called a steamroller duck. It was a whole duck that had been plucked and then perhaps smoked before being pressed flat.

Inviting small side roads which climbed steeply up the side of the hill seemed to be the home of particular trades. One was the preserve of the ivory carvers at whose skill I could only marvel. From a piece of tusk they could carve a devil ball inside which they had carved up to six freely moving inner balls of diminishing size. The outer ball and all the inner balls except the innermost had several perfectly circular holes in them allowing the carver access to the ball below. Usually an intricate classical picture was carved on the outer ball, but I was told that this was often done to cover defects and that the most valuable balls were those which were perfect spheres without ornamentation. It was fascinating to watch the craftsmen at work. They used what looked like miniature scythes to cut the inner balls free and they all held their work close to their face. Next to the street of the ivory carvers was that of the jade specialists who seemed to be able to shape jade into the most complex configurations. It did not appeal to me as much as the ivory but there were some beautiful and costly models of horses, lions and other animals which took my eye.

Next to the street of the jade merchants came that of the leather workers, followed by the street of flowers. It was so steep that it was a series of steps, with each side covered with banks of gorgeous flowers. It was a sight to behold and clearly drew the attention of the local artists who hung around trying to sell their paintings of the scene. Further along there were a number of large, crowded markets of which the most fascinating was the bird market. Here there were hundreds of birds for sale, together with cages in which to house them and stuff with which to feed them. The latter included what looked like live grasshoppers, tiny mice and even snakes. The place was always crowded and as in all other markets very noisy as customers argued with vendors over prices, whilst stallholders shouted their wares.

Fortunately, however, there were places around the island that were not noisy and had a relaxed almost resort-like atmosphere. Repulse Bay with its prestigious Repulse Bay Hotel was the best known. We were not allowed in the hotel but there was a fine beach there where we sometimes went for a swim. One day when I was there an elderly gentleman told me how the bay got its derogatory name. Apparently when the island was ceded to the British the bay was home to bands of pirates and other undesirables who were well dug in and defied all efforts to dislodge them. Finally the Governor ordered the Navy to send in a battleship and bombard the area. The ship chosen for this purpose was HMS *Repulse*, whose efforts were successful, so much so that the grateful colonists named the bay after the ship

Although the beach at Repulse Bay was good I preferred the one at Big Wave Bay. We had discovered how to get there using the local bus service and it became a favorite haunt, especially during the summer months. The waves there are not really big waves; indeed, a surfer would probably not recognize them as waves. They are about the size found on a calm day rolling onto beaches along the English Channel and there was very little undertow. With water temperatures in the 70 to 75 degrees Fahrenheit range, this made for comfortable bathing. When air temperatures were in the high 90s during the summer, with humidity to match, Big Wave Bay was a good place to be. It also had a facility not to be found at Repulse Bay, which we called Madam Chang's Beach Hut Service. As soon as one arrived at the beach a little old Chinese lady dressed all in black, would appear out of nowhere and for the princely sum of two Hong Kong dollars would promptly erect a small tent in which we could change and leave our clothes. She would then squat outside the tent and guard all our gear whilst we swam and played volleyball. When we returned and changed back into uniform she would dismantle the tent and disappear with it. We never did discover where she came from or where she went — she just appeared and disappeared. There were Chinese restaurants in both Repulse and Big Wave Bays, and thousands in Hong Kong and Kowloon on the mainland, but with one exception I never went into any of them. In retrospect, it seems such a wastcd opportunity not to have sampled some of the world's finest cuisine whilst stationed in Hong Kong but somehow it never occurred to either my friends or myself to try it. I suppose because we were English we thought that we only ate English food, although the one exception was a restaurant in Aberdeen. At that time Aberdeen was a fishing village on the seaward side of the island where a small ancillary naval dockyard had been established. There we came across a restaurant which displayed in its window and around the sides of its dining room large glass tanks full of sea water in which dozens of fish swam around. Perhaps it was seeing the fish and thinking of fish and chips that overcame our reluctance to enter a Chinese restaurant — anyway, we went in. The waiters showed no surprise at seeing us and showed us to a table. Our particular waiter then indicated that we should go up and choose a fish. After some hesitation we did this, whereupon the waiter, using a small hand-held net, caught the fish and then kept asking what was obviously a question, but we could not understand it at the time so he gave up and proceeded to the kitchen to have our chosen fish cooked. I learned later that what he was asking was how we wanted our fish cooked. Needless to say we did not get fish and chips but the meal when it came was excellent and we went back to that restaurant a number of times. I recall that I even developed a preferred cooking method in which the fish was coated with a thin toffee-like glaze, but I cannot remember now what it was called.

When I first arrived in Hong Kong it was crowded with refugees from China fleeing the Japanese, and there were extremes of wealth and poverty — the former in the hands of privileged Europeans and Chinese, and the latter among the refugees. Thousands were homeless and sleeping on the streets, and the efforts of the government relief agencies were constantly undermined by fresh waves of would-be immigrants who braved great hardships to reach the safe haven of Hong Kong. The homeless problem was particularly evident in the vicinity of the China Fleet Club, the principal Service recreational club for noncommissioned ranks. It boasted billiard tables, table tennis tables and a huge bar where tombola (aka bingo) was played every night.[3] The club was situated in the centre of Wanchai, which at that time not only contained thousands of homeless people but was also home to sleazy dance halls, brothels, gambling joints and grossly overcrowded apartments. The homeless crowded the sidewalks, sitting or lying on pieces of cardboard or thin bamboo matting. They hung around the streetlights and many had the unfortunate habit of noisily clearing their throats and spitting indiscriminately on the ground (at first I thought that they must be suffering from bronchitis or even tuberculosis but soon learned that the habit was prevalent throughout many parts of China). When one approached the Fleet Club, beggars, rickshaw coolies, hawkers and prostitutes assailed you, the latter shouting, "You come my house, Jack, five dollah." On my very first shore leave, when I was escorted by a leading hand intent on showing me

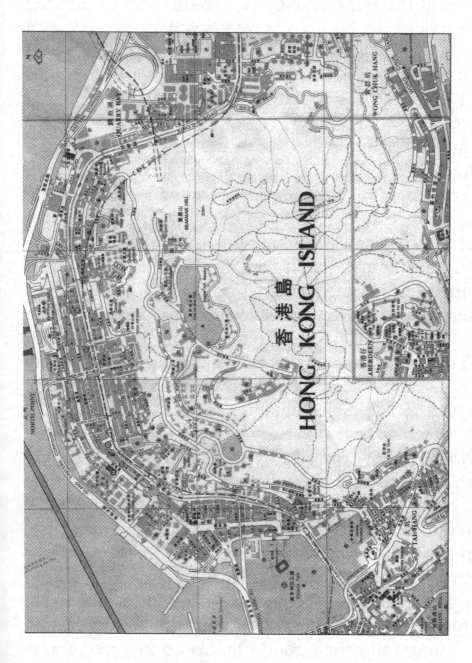

Hong Kong Island

the way to the Fleet Club, both my upper arms were grabbed at the same time by two young women offering their services. As both arms were swollen and sore as a result of the vaccination and inoculations I had received earlier in the day, I found these attentions painful and I fear I was not too polite in declining the proffered services.

I found the plight of the homeless disconcerting during my early days in the Colony. I could not help feeling sorry, for example, for a woman carrying one child strapped to her back, another cradled in one arm whilst she held out a begging bowl with her free hand, and a third small child clinging to her threadbare clothing, the quartet squatting on a piece of cardboard at the edge of a crowded sidewalk, looking as though they were not destined to remain long in this world. Then there were the very elderly people, some relatively well dressed but forced to sleep on the pavement; and there were children, presumably orphaned or abandoned, who were trying to survive by begging. Taken individually they evoked a wave of sympathy and pity, but there were so many of them that collectively they were overwhelming and one's mind moved to block them out. Before long I became like everybody else, accepting them as part of the norm, and as there was nothing I could do about them, I tended to ignore them. I also accepted as normal something which today I would find intolerable — the fact that I was denied entry into all the good hotels and restaurants patronized by Europeans. They all had a sign outside which read "Non commissioned service personnel,

Chinese and Dogs not admitted". Even on the Peak tram which some of us used on a daily basis, non-commissioned ranks were not allowed to sit in the forward section reserved for "Europeans Only" — we rode with the Chinese in the rear section.

By way of compensation the Navy had superb sports facilities designed to accommodate the whole of the pre-war China Fleet, nearly all of which had been sent for service in the Atlantic and the Mediterranean. All that was left of that once mighty armada were three First World War turtle-back destroyers of some 900 tons (HMS *Thracian*, HMS *Thanet* and HMS *Scout*), three Insectclass river gunboats (HMS *Moth*, HMS *Cicala* and HMS *Tern*), one gunboat of a different class, HMS *Robin*, and the Second Motor Torpedo Boat Flotilla (seven Vickers boats and two Thornecroft, all of which were desperately short of spares). There was therefore an abundance of facilities for personnel remaining on the station and one could participate in almost any sport you might care to mention. Whilst football was the most popular among the younger naval personnel, there were a surprising number who played tennis and I joined them (whilst I liked football watchkeeping made it difficult to commit to team fixtures, whereas one could always find somebody free to play tennis). The sports centre contained a large number of fine hard tennis courts, and a vacant one could always be found whenever you arrived there. Fortunately there were also plenty of showers because playing in the summer heat certainly made you perspire. To cope with it the standard drill when we finished playing was to take a cold shower and then go to the bar wearing only a loose-fitting pair of shorts, there to partake of two pints of ginger beer shandy which almost immediately reappeared as more perspiration. Then, when ready to go, we would take a hot shower before changing back into uniform.

If sports did not appeal to one, the Colony had other attractions. There were air-conditioned cinemas that showed films direct from Hollywood. For those who could stand it there was Chinese opera — I tried it once but only managed to survive for an hour before the noise drove me out. There was also horse racing at the Happy Valley Racecourse on the outskirts of the city. The Yeoman of my watch was an enthusiastic racegoer and on three occasions he persuaded the whole watch to go to the races with him. The Chinese love to gamble and horse racing appealed to all levels of society so that the car parks were crowded with every type of vehicle from Rolls-Royces to rickshaws. The rich had their boxes, others the members' stands and enclosures, whilst the rest, including us, crowded the public areas. The racing was conducted under the auspices of the Royal Hong Kong Jockey Club and was similar to what I had seen in England. There were bookies, a Tote, tick-tack men and tipsters, but there were two differences from an English race meeting. The first was that the horses were not horses at all — they were large ponies about the size used in polo. The other was that they ran the wrong way round. Instead of running anti-clockwise round the track, they ran clockwise. This did not detract from the excitement, however, for we had a small bet on most races. We all put ten dollars into a kitty and took turns in choosing which pony we would back to win, and which to back for a place. The bets were usually five dollars and we ran out of cash before the racing ended on the first two occasions I visited the track. On the last occasion, though, thanks largely to a bet on the field at fifty to one placed by one of the leading hands, we came away with a small profit.

In addition to the regular entertainments, band concerts were held from time to time. I have good reason to remember one that took place in September 1941. It was held on the Hong Kong Club's cricket ground, which in those days was situated in the middle of Victoria. (It was a beautifully maintained pitch that regrettably no longer exists, having become a park known as "Chater Gardens", a small oasis of green tranquillity in a noisy stone and tarmac desert.) Drinks were on sale in the marquee but to get them one had to have a book of tickets, costing HK$5. A book contained four tickets, each of which was good for one drink. The concert came right at the end of the month and the four of us that were attending could only scrape together five dollars between us (pay day being another two days away). So all we bought was one book but then it started to rain and people began to run to the Hong Kong Club for shelter. As he passed, the Port Signal Officer threw me a couple of books and told me to make use of them. Others followed his lead and by the time the stampede out of the gates was over we had collected twenty-two books. When we reached the

35

drinks marquee the only thing left was Scotch and crème de menthe. We drank the Scotch — I don't remember how many, nor do I recall how we made our way back to the bungalow on the Peak. I do remember, however, that when I got into bed it started to pitch as if we were at sea, and that with a great effort of will I made it swing to left and right; when it reached maximum altitude on a left-hand roll I leaned out of the open window and was violently sick. For the next few days everything I ate tasted of whiskey and I was so put off the stuff that twenty-five years passed before I drank any again.

The band concert was one of the few occasions when one entered the world of the civilian European population. Another was at the annual Service tennis championships, which were held over two days on the courts of the prestigious Ladies' Recreation Club on the Peak. Despite the fact that the majority of European women were supposed to have been evacuated from the Colony to Australia early in 1940, there remained a number of wives of senior officials and other ladies who for some reason had been allowed to, or had elected to remain. The Ladies' Recreation Club was therefore still very active and although few if any of its members attended the Service champion- ships, those of us involved in the competition not only had the benefit of playing on the club's splendid courts, but also of using the club's catering facilities as well. We enjoyed drinking tea from bone china cups and eating sandwiches of which Fortnum and Mason would have been proud. It was a pleasant change from naval cuisine and a reminder of what it used to be like at home.

The only other occasion I can recall being involved in any civilian operation was at the Governor's Ball held in the Rose Room of the Peninsular Hotel. It was the social event of the season, attended by everybody who was anybody in Hong Kong and not the kind of event to which the lower forms of animal life expected to be invited. However I happened to be in the main signal office one morning when the Port Signal Officer unexpectedly burst in. He advanced on the Chief Yeoman saying, "Chief, in my hand are three tickets to the Governor's Ball tonight. The Governor himself has had them sent over in recognition of the service we provide his office with instructions that they are to go to three communications ratings." He swung round and his eyes alighted on the three of us who had just come off the all-night watch: a petty officer, a leading hand and me. "These three have just volunteered, Chief," he said. "Have them on inspection at nineteen hundred hours, dress of the day Number One and I hold you responsible for seeing that they attend and behave themselves." With that he stormed out. The unflappable Chief Yeoman forestalled any protest from us by saying, "You heard what he said, fall in for inspection on board *Tamar* at nineteen hundred tonight and thank God he didn't order me to go with you."

When the news of our predicament flashed around the mess decks there were a few ribald comments, but for the most part the reaction was the same as the Chief Yeoman's — rather you than me, Jack. Whilst the Petty

37

Officer and I were not enthralled by the prospect of attending the ball, we were not apprehensive, but the Leading Hand was. He had been an orphan, brought up in one of Dr Bernardo's orphanages, and had joined the Navy as a boy entrant at age fourteen. He had never known any life outside the confines of the service and the thought of being catapulted into high society filled him with dread. He tried to bribe others to take his place but there were no takers and so he had to join the Petty Officer and me when we duly paraded on board *Tamar* at 1900 hours. We were inspected not only by the Chief Yeoman but also by the Master at Arms himself. He told us that the reputation of the Navy was in our hands and that if we did not behave ourselves he personally would ensure that we never had shore leave again. He also said he was sending two members of the shore patrol with us on the trip across the harbour. I suspect he sent them to make sure that we did not chicken out at the last minute for they accompanied us all the way to the Peninsular and watched us go in.

It was just eight o'clock in the evening when the three of us, dressed in our Sunday best, walked up the steps to the gilded doors of the Colony's premier hotel. The Rose Room at the Peninsular was on what the English called the first and the Americans the second floor. It was really two rooms connected by a long narrow chamber in which, for the occasion of the ball, the band was located. Dancers could dance from one room to the other and both were sumptuously decorated with masses of flowers. The band was playing when we arrived as an attendant took our hats and another our invitation cards. Waiters repeatedly offered us drinks and canapés but nobody came and spoke to us and we stood like wallflowers on the periphery of the activities. The band, which was from the Royal Scots military band, was good and I quite enjoyed listening to it and watching the dancers. After a couple of hours though I was tired of just standing there and added my voice to that of the Leading Hand who for the last hour or so had been loudly contending that we had done our duty and it was "time to get the hell out of here". I think the Petty Officer had just about reached the same conclusion when the Master of Ceremonies announced that the next dance would be a "ladies choice". Three ladies swept across the dance floor towards us and we were all invited to dance. It was the Governor's wife who took me in tow, charmingly waving aside my protest that I did not know this dance. "Just follow me," she said, "I will lead" and lead she did — despite my clumsy footwork we danced well around the floor. She was what my mother would have termed a well-built woman and in her full-length spring-green evening gown was an impressive figure. She had the knack of putting one at ease so that as she chatted I began to relax and took a quick look around to see how my companions were faring. The Petty Officer seemed to be doing well but I noticed that the Leading Hand and his partner had given up and retired to the sidelines. I thought that I would be joining him soon as the dance was coming to an end when suddenly there was a loud ripping noise and looking down I saw that the front panel of my partner's dress had been torn

39

away at the waist and lay on the floor where it was firmly anchored by my foot. I had stepped on her dress just as she had swung away. I was mortified, and wished the floor would open up and swallow me, but she was magnificent. "Oh dear," she said, "never mind, don't worry, I never did like this dress and now that old skinflint of a husband of mine will just have to buy me a new one." Somehow I got off the floor and the three of us made what we hoped was a dignified if somewhat hasty departure. The next day when asked how we had fared at the ball no mention was made of the incident with the dress — we just said that it was all right and that the food and drinks were terrific. I therefore thought that it was unlikely the matter would reach the ears of my masters. Two days later, however, as I came off watch the Chief Yeoman called me into his inner sanctum and with an absolutely deadpan face said, "I am surprised that a young man of your upbringing and education should go round ripping off ladies' skirts in the middle of a dance floor; it is not a very gentlemanly thing to do. Do not let me hear of you doing it again."

Notes:

1. "Three-badge AB". Able Seaman who had been awarded three good conduct stripes, one stripe being awarded for every three years of "undetected crime".
2. Admiralty London. During the hours of darkness radio signals could be sent directly from the Admiralty transmitters in London to the naval radio station on Stonecutters Island, and vice versa. The technique used involved reducing all information to

a series of numbers recorded on a tape. This tape was then transmitted at very high speed, and the receiving station used a device to effectively slow down the incoming tape and print out a hard copy of the original transmission.

3. Tombola, or bingo, as it is sometimes called, was the only game of chance permitted in the Royal Navy. It was played on board the *Tamar*. Whenever a sailor went on shore leave from a warship moored in a harbour, he had to go on the "liberty boat" which departed the ship at specific times. We had to follow this routine on the *Tamar* even though she was alongside the dock and all we had to do was to walk down the gangway. The reason for this procedure was that all men had to be inspected for being properly dressed etc. by the Duty Regulating Petty Officer before being permitted to proceed ashore. On the *Tamar* the drill was to be at the assembly point half an hour before the "boat" was due to depart. During that half hour tombola was played with the Regulating Petty Officer calling the numbers. Cards were 10 Hong Kong cents each and on my very first trip ashore I won one dollar ten cents!

CHAPTER
THREE

On Coming of Age

Whilst I had been enjoying the Hong Kong high life, changes were taking place in the naval garrison. Just as the ships had been sent to home waters, so went nearly all Hong Kong's anti-aircraft guns and anything else that would be useful to help replace the equipment lost at Dunkirk. Over time the men went too. Rear Admiral Peters went home in the spring of 1941 and was replaced by Commodore Collinson. The experienced petty officers, leading hands and ratings of all categories who were in Hong Kong when I first arrived began to disappear. They were replaced, at least in part, by people like me, Hostilities Only personnel. Included among them was a new breed of animal — coders — and with their arrival I did get a few welcome changes of duties for a while.

A two-day beach landing exercise on one of the outer islands was arranged and a signalman was required to facilitate communications between the Beachmaster, a Royal Marines major, and the ships. I was obviously not the first choice for the job, so a leading hand from one of the other watches was given the job. On the morning of the second day of the exercise when I had just come on watch the Chief Yeoman said, "Mathews is sick so you are to go on the Landing Exercise. There is a motor boat waiting alongside at the mole and the Major is already aboard. You had better get down there fast." I thought they must be short of skilled operators if they were sending me.

When we arrived at the beach I soon realized that the chief knew what he was doing — I did not have to do much signalling. The two destroyers (*Thracian* and *Thanet*) involved in the operation came into the bay, their upper decks crowded with soldiers, and dropped anchor about 300 yards from the beach. The soldiers then boarded the ships' whalers and were rowed ashore by the boats' crews. All I had to do was read a signal from the ships that indicated the boats were underway, record the time, send one back and again record the time when they reached the beach. The Major would look at the elapsed time and almost invariably say, "Too damned long." The exercise went on all day and I tried to help out by pulling the boats up the beach and pushing them back when they were returning to the destroyers. The Major was never happy about the time it took to land the troops but at sundown the exercise was ended and everybody was transported back to the Naval Dockyard in Hong Kong. The next day I found that I had large blisters on all my toes and had to report to the sick bay. The Sick Berth Petty Officer there took one look at my feet and said, "You must have been on the landing exercise skylark. Your pal is in the first bed, you get in the second." "My pal" was the Leading Hand who had been on the beach the first day of the exercise and he too had blistered feet. We were told that our feet are the one part of the body that are rarely exposed to the sun for any length of time, so when you spend nearly twelve hours in full sun in bare feet, wading in and out of salt water, they react. We were both kept in the sick bay for a week.

Shortly after this incident I was offered the chance to go out with the MTBs on a night patrol, which I gladly accepted. We left the MTB base in Kowloon and proceeded out to sea via the Lei Yue Mun Channel. As we passed the Cape D'Aguilar Signal Station located on the top of the cliffs that bordered the channel, a signal light suddenly flashed directly at us and for the first and only time I read a shore-to-ship signal. It was only two words in plain language: "Bismarck sunk".

There were three boats in the patrol and we headed in the direction of the anticipated course of an Italian armed merchantman which was known to have left Yokohama in Japan two days previously, heading south. The plan was for two boats to patrol one side of the anticipated course of the merchantman whilst the third went to the other side where it would heave to and remain silent. Then if the patrolling boats sighted the enemy they would attack, and whilst the opposition's attention was concentrated on the attacking boats the third one would sneak in out of the darkness and launch its torpedoes from close range. Unfortunately for me the boat I was on was the third one. I had enjoyed being on the MTBs when they were moving but when they were not and the only motion was rolling from one wave to the next I became seasick. The rolling went on all night so I was very glad when dawn came with no sign of the enemy and we were recalled to base.

At about the time of the MTB incident arrangements were being made to assist the Hong Kong Royal Naval Volunteer Reserve (HKRNVR), which comprised English officers and Chinese ratings. It practised at weekends and some of the senior ratings from the Signal Office were sent to train the local lads. To my surprise I was even called upon to help and was sent to be the communications rating on a minelayer. The *Man Yeung*, for that was what she was called, was no ordinary minelayer having spent most of her life as a car ferry plowing across Hong Kong harbour. The Navy had requisitioned her, laid three sets of narrow-gauge rails along her car deck, put a compass on her bridge and classified her as a fleet auxiliary. Except for the skipper, a lieutenant commander, and myself, the crew were all Chinese, most of whom had been on her when she was a ferry, including the coxswain who had been her peacetime skipper. He was an interesting character who was taller than most Chinese and about forty years old. He spoke some English and came from Aberdeen where his family had been fishermen for many generations. He knew the waters around Hong Kong like the back of his hand and could handle the ex-car ferry with great expertise. I learned sufficient Chinese words and expressions from him to communicate to the crew a few basic orders such as "push the next mine overboard now". That particular instruction was important because there was no communication system between the bridge and the car deck. The Navy had installed a buzzer but the skipper did not trust that and so I became the great communicator. The bridge was some 15 feet above the car deck and when at sea the skipper, the coxswain and I were stationed there. When we were on what the CO called a drop run (i.e. laying the mines), he would have a stopwatch in his hand and I would take station down the ladder leading to the car deck to the point where my head was just above the floor of the wheelhouse/bridge. The skipper would raise his arm to tell me to stand by and drop it as a signal to lay a mine. I would then slide down the rest of the ladder to the car deck and shout to the crew to push one over the stern, a process easily performed by pushing the mine off the end of the track on which it had rested onto what had once been the *Man Yeung*'s car loading ramp, which sloped down to the water. Of course, during these exercises real mines were not dropped. Instead we used small weighted trolleys to which were attached a buoy. These floated up so that at the end of a run we could tell how accurately they had been laid and whether the distance between each mine was what it should be. Having completed a run we would turn round, and recover the buoys and their trolleys. It always interested me to see how the coxswain dealt with the skipper's instructions. Before we set out the Lieutenant Commander would get out the charts and show the coxswain where he wanted to go. The coxswain would take a cursory glance at the chart and without any more instruction take us exactly to the spot. There the skipper would instruct him to steer a specific course, which did not mean much to a man who had spent the greater part of his life at sea without any need for a compass. The skipper knew this so after giving the course instruction he would always add, "Steer for that point." The same instruction method was used when we operated at night only then it was "Steer for that light." I wondered how we would get on if there was a war and a blackout was imposed. In the event I need not have worried as the old coxswain could operate in thick fog — a blackout did not worry him. I once asked him how he seemed to know where he was all the time, even on a moonless night in a blackout, whereas I frequently lost track of our position. He answered in Cantonese and I could not interpret it but one of the Chinese ratings told me, "He smells the sea."

All these new experiences made life interesting. We were not paid much but everything was so cheap that we wanted for little. One worried about what might be happening to one's family at home but a first-class mail service (which came via the USA and across the Pacific on the President Lines fast liners) and a mother that wrote every week kept me well informed. The war news was not good but I never doubted that England would prevail in the end; it was just going to take longer! As 1941 progressed, however, the Far East situation deteriorated with the Japanese and the Americans engaging in verbal warfare. Crises began to develop with monotonous regularity (invariably at weekends) but as nothing concrete ever seemed to happen; in time we tended to ignore them, particularly when in

November 1941 three other matters captured our attention.

The first was the arrival in the late summer of 1941 of a new C-in-C, Major General Maltby. He took a while to review the military situation and then early in November ordered the two British Army units stationed in the Colony to change places. This meant that the 2nd Battalion of the Middlesex Regiment, which together with Rajput and Punjabi battalions from the Indian Army had been guarding the Kowloon/China border for some four years, had to take over the defence of Hong Kong island, while the battalion of Royal Scots, which for several years had had that responsibility, had to join the Rajputs and Punjabis and take over the defence of the border with China. The justification the C-in-C gave for the move was that both battalions had been left in one position for too long and had become stale. He was probably correct in his assessment of the situation and in ordinary circumstances the decision to move his troops would have been a good one. Unfortunately circumstances were not normal and the decision proved disastrous — within two weeks of the exchange being made the Japanese attacked long before either battalion was fully familiar with its new area.[1]

The second event of note in that autumn of 1941 was the arrival of Canadian troops. Two battalions arrived, one each from the Royal Rifles of Canada and the Winnipeg Grenadiers. They came in two New Zealand liners accompanied by HMS *Danae*,[2] a First World War light cruiser that had been used as a RNVR training vessel between the wars. Much to the disgust of the Canadians during the voyage they were fed a diet of mutton, something most of them had never seen before and never wanted to again. They all seemed very tall and were anxious to do their stuff, but they had no heavy weapons. Rifles, some mortars and light machine guns were all they had and unfortunately it was much the same for the rest of the troops in Hong Kong. In later years, reading Churchill's history of the war, I discovered that it had been decided early in 1940 that the UK forces were stretched so thin that none could be spared to strengthen the garrison at Hong Kong. In the event of war in the Far East, therefore, the Colony could probably not avoid capture and accordingly all useful equipment would be removed and only a token force left there. The logic of that decision is irrefutable and accounted for the removal of the ships and many guns from the island, so why at the eleventh hour and fifty-ninth minute was this group of partly trained and totally inexperienced Canadians sent to Hong Kong in direct contradiction of that logic? It seems to me that the stupidity of the move was matched only by the decision to send boatloads of troops into Singapore Island less than ten days before it capitulated.

The third and by far the most important event of the season (for me at least) was my twenty-first birthday on 22 November. My mother had sent a birthday cake, for which she must have used four weeks of her sugar and butter rations; it came in a biscuit tin the lid of which my father had soldered on. This kept it in good condition and the cake was much appreciated by members of the Peak mess. The planning for the birthday party had been very thorough as it was my intention, and that of my friends, to risk court martial and change into civilian clothes, which would enable us to circumvent the "No dogs" and "Officers only" restrictions at the best hotels and restaurants (to be seen out of uniform was a court-marshal offence). In order to do this we made arrangements with one of Mr Shan Tuck's many relatives, who owned a tailor's shop on Nathan Road in Kowloon. From him we rented suitable clothing, took them to the YMCA where we had booked rooms, changed and went out in our hired splendour. The plan was to cross to Hong Kong, return to Kowloon on the last ferry, spend what was left of the night at the YM, change back into uniform and report back on board as usual at 0700 hours, having left the civilian gear to be collected by one of Mr Tuck's innumerable relatives. In the event, we stuck to the plan but an unforeseen happening momentarily cast a shadow over the evening. As we came off the Star Ferry on the Hong Kong side, resplendent in sports coats and grey flannels, there waiting to board the ferry was "God", the Regulating Chief Petty Officer (the Master at Arms) and although he continued on his way and boarded the ferry there could be no doubt that he had seen us. It was decided that there was not much that could be done about it. The next day would be the day of reckoning so we might as well make the most of the night — and we did. Although we encountered one or two queer looks at some of the points of call nobody forbade entry and we had a great time. The only place we chickened out on was the Hong Kong Hotel and its famous "Grips" bar. Two of our party were newly promoted Petty Officers, Fisher and Simmons, and they warned us that if we went in there we might meet some officers to whom we were well known. At the time I think the rest of us were sufficiently inebriated that we would have pressed on, but fortunately wisdom prevailed and probably just as well, for there waiting for me at the head of *Tamar*'s gangway when I reported in at 0700 the next morning was "God", immaculate as always in a spotless, freshly pressed uniform. This is it, I thought. He will have me in the brig in no time flat. But no, as I stepped on to the deck, he said, "Good morning, Wort. Have a good run ashore last night?"

"Yes Master," I stuttered.

"I am glad," he said. "You are only twenty-one once, you know; you have got to make the most of it."

It was then I realized "God" was human after all and relief flooded over me. Particularly so because the previous evening I had completely forgotten that two days earlier I had been summoned to the Commodore's office and informed that the Port Signal Officer was prepared to recommend that I attend Officer Training School in accordance with a new program contained in an AFO (Admiralty Fleet Order). Unfortunately events moved too swiftly for anything to come of it.

As November neared its end several Japanese troopships were sighted going up the Pearl River towards Canton. There was a general feeling of tension in the air. Signals were received saying that the battleship HMS *Prince of Wales* and battlecruiser

51

HMS *Repulse* had arrived in Singapore and that more troops were being sent there. It seemed that the balloon was about to go up, but we had had so many false alarms in the past that despite the ominous signs we were still not completely convinced that this was the real thing. The Americans and the Japanese were still talking and high-level meetings were to be held in Washington. No "stand to" orders were issued and life went on as usual until the morning of 8 December. I was on the Peak tram travelling down to report at the dockyard at 0700 when I heard a "crump crump" coming from the direction of the airport at Kai Tack. Black smoke was rising and an ancient Walrus single-engine flying boat was staggering into the air, but a swarm of small fighters attacked it and it fell in flames into the sea. The long-threatened war in the Far East had begun.

Notes:

1. I was told by some Royal Scots in the prison camp that they were so unfamiliar with their positions in the New Territories that one of their warrant officers was wandering around the border area trying to find his unit when the Japanese attack began. He was the Bandmaster and had conducted the Royal Scots Dance Band (the same one that had played at the Governor's Ball) at an event in Hong Kong during the evening of Sunday, 7 December. It was nearly 4.00 a.m. before he got back to the border area still in his dress uniform. Although he heard music well

enough to be a bandmaster, for some peculiar reason he was partially deaf to all other sounds; whilst searching for his unit he apparently did not hear the Japanese troops advancing across the border and thus became the first casualty of the war in Hong Kong

2. HMS *Danae* and the two New Zealand Line vessels that had transported the Canadians from Vancouver to Hong Kong departed within a week of arrival. Before they sailed, however, a requirement was posted for a Signalman Trained Operator for service in the Middle East; the man was to take passage on the *Danae*. Warrant Officer Mitchell, the senior Yeoman, asked for volunteers and whilst I was still thinking about it one of the regulars stepped forward. I have often wondered what would have happened if I had volunteered first.

CHAPTER
FOUR

On the Battle for
Hong Kong

As far as Hong Kong was concerned the fighting war lasted seventeen days, two weeks longer than the Japanese invaders had anticipated. I spent the first seven of those days on the minelayer *Man Yeung*. We loaded up with the real thing at the armaments depot on Stonecutters Island, and laid them around the island and in the approach channels to the harbour. We were buzzed a few times by Japanese floatplanes but they did not fire on us. I can only assume that we were mistaken for a normal ferry not worthy of consideration by the aviators of Nippon. Nevertheless, bearing in mind all the high explosives sitting on what had been the car deck it was somewhat scary when they dived at us. Equally disconcerting was the fact that on the horizon, well out of the range of the coastal gun batteries, three Japanese cruisers could be seen patrolling. If we could see them presumably they could see us and what we were doing. I expected them to come in after us at any moment but they did not and we completed four days of minelaying operations virtually unchallenged before returning to the Victoria Naval Dockyard.

We had gone there on the morning of 9 December so that the skipper could report to the Naval Headquarters. Whilst there he learned that one of our three destroyers, HMS *Thanet*,[1] had left during the night (so had the American river gunboat USS *Guam* which had been stationed in Hong Kong). Nobody seemed to know where she was bound but Singapore was the most popular guess. Whilst we were at the dockyard, two security vans in the livery of the Hong Kong and Shanghai Bank drew up. Men emerged from them armed with side arms and proceeded to unload wooden boxes which they carried to HMS *Scout* which had come alongside the dockyards outer wall.[2] They were obviously very heavy boxes because although they were only about 15 inches long and roughly 6 to 8 inches wide and deep, with thick rope handles on each side, it took two men to lift each one. The handlers had great difficulty in manoeuvring the boxes down the narrow gangway from the dockside to the ship's quarterdeck, and it took them almost an hour to unload all the boxes and stow them below deck on the *Scout*. She sailed that night taking with her what was obviously bullion from the Hong Kong and Shanghai Bank and, as the *Thanet* had already departed, any hope we had of getting off the island seemed pretty slim. The same day the *Scout* left, our one remaining destroyer, HMS *Thracian*,[3] was moved to the Aberdeen naval base on the seaward side of the island, as were the MTBs. Two large passenger planes belonging to China Airlines were seen to leave Kai Tak airport one evening, presumably carrying VIPs, thereby emphasizing our sense of isolation. Over the next few days every time we returned to the dockyard the news seemed to get worse and worse. The Japs were advancing in the Philippines and appeared to be moving rapidly down the Malayan peninsular from their initial landing at Kota Baru on the north-east coast. It was said that the American Pacific Fleet had been destroyed at Pearl Harbor. A plain language signal was then received from HMS *Repulse* stating that HMS *Prince of Wales* had sunk having suffered five torpedo hits, that the *Repulse* herself had been hit by four torpedoes and although sinking was fighting on. Clearly any hope of seaborne relief was out of the question and we were very much on our own.

In our own local conflict the Japanese had crossed the border in the early hours of 8 December and although delayed by the demolition of bridges and roads, by the second day of the war approached the thinly held Gin Drinkers Line which stretched for 11 miles across the narrowest part of the New Territories. This first line of defence was manned by the Royal Scots, the Punjabis and the Rajputs. Its only strongpoint was the Redoubt at Shing Mun, which essentially consisted of five pillboxes connected by a series of tunnels. It was in the Royal Scots' section of the line and in a night operation the Japanese managed to isolate it and attacked it with specially trained, silent-footed assault troops. They somehow managed to slip past the Scots patrols and outer defences before dropping explosives down the ventilation shafts of the pillboxes. The fall of the Redoubt broke the back of the only line of defence on the mainland and once that happened our forces began an orderly withdrawal to Hong Kong Island. The Rajputs in particular fought a stubborn rearguard action but by the end of the first week of war all the Colony's military personnel had been evacuated to the island, and at 2.30a.m. on the morning following the completion of the evacuation, the *Man Yeung* (now bereft of mines) was ordered to proceed to Kowloon to pick up any stragglers. No one knew for sure whether a Japanese advance guard had already reached the Kowloon waterfront, so it was with some degree of apprehension we approached the Star Ferry pier. The night binoculars with which we studied the pier and its immediate surroundings revealed no sign of movement, nor was there any sound — the place was ominously silent. So we drifted slowly in ready to go full astern at the slightest suspicious movement. I half expected to be fired on from the adjacent buildings but nothing happened and all was quiet as we came alongside the pier and secured. We waited for about half an hour and as all appeared quiet I was sent ashore "to see what you can find". It was an eerie experience. In the immediate viscinity of the pier it was very dark and as silent as a grave, but in the distance I could hear rifle fire and some low thumping noises. Keeping close to the buildings I walked a few hundred yards along the familiar and normally brilliantly lit and crowded waterfront, past Canton Street, until I came to the YMCA building. Nothing

57

moved even when I called out, "Any more for the Skylark?" so I went back to the pier and reported that I could find nobody. The skipper decided we would wait for a couple of hours and if things remained quiet I should go ashore again for one last look round whilst it was still dark. It was a long two hours whilst we talked only in whispers and I sensed that the crew was getting jumpy. There had been no movement we could see and no sound we could hear so the skipper told me that I had better go and have one more quick look round before we left. The result was the same as on the first trip; I found no stragglers, even though this time I went past the YMCA and the Peninsular Hotel to the corner of Nathan Road. Standing there, the rifle fire and thumping noises seemed closer than on my first sortie. I made my way back to the pier without seeing anyone but when a small animal (probably a cat or a large rat) ran across the pavement in front of me just as I reached Canton Street I nearly jumped out of my skin. With dawn not far off it was deemed unsafe to stay much longer, and at about 5.30a.m. we cast off and returned to the naval dockyard in Victoria central. Later that day the skipper and I were ordered to report to Naval Headquarters and the coxswain was told to take the *Man Yeung* round to the dockyard at Aberdeen. As I left the ex-car ferry the coxswain touched my arm and wished me good luck. I never saw him or the *Man Yeung* again. None of the Chinese crew ever turned up in the prison camp. I think and I certainly hope that before the surrender they shed their uniforms and slipped back into civilian life. They may well have rejoined the fishing fleet which the Japanese permitted to continue operating in order to help supply the Colony with food.

The Japanese were not seen on the Kowloon waterfront until the evening of the day we had left it. They spent the next two days dragging their light artillery into position together with a whole battery of searchlights. They then began to shell the island and at the same time intensified their bombing raids. Those made by squadrons of twin-engined aircraft flying in tight formation at great height were not very effective, even though they were made every one and a half hours during the day (we surmised that this interval was the time it took the aircraft to execute their bombing run, return to their base airfield near Canton, refuel and rearm, and return to Hong Kong for another raid). On the other hand raids by small fighter-bombers mainly against shipping were highly successful. Much of the shipping in the harbour was sunk by dive-bombing attacks and the only craft that could defend themselves were the tiny river gunboats. Their main armament could be raised to a high angle and doubled as anti-aircraft guns (few of which were available to the defenders on the island); with their shallow draft and triple rudder system they were highly manoeuvrable. They were constantly under attack during daylight hours and seemed to constitute an irresistible challenge to the Japanese Air Force which attacked them when there were plenty of easier and strategically more important targets available. They bombarded Japanese land forces on the mainland and on the island and lead

59

Kowloon

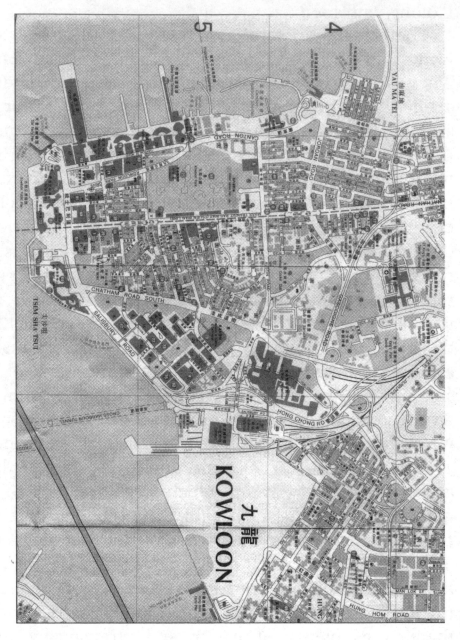

a charmed life. Their captains lay on a deck chair on the bridge with binoculars in hand and as they saw the attacking aircraft release its bomb ordered a rapid course change. As those gunboats could turn in their own length they were well clear before the bomb plunged into the sea. Between them they shot down at least two aircraft and probably damaged a great deal more. One by one, however, they were sunk but it was not until the very last day of the battle that the last remaining gunboat, HMS *Cicala*, was sunk by a squadron of dive-bombers whilst she was shelling Japanese troops in the Repulse Bay area.

The shelling of the island was not as severe as anticipated even though it was done at virtually point-blank range from the Kowloon quayside across the narrowest part of the harbour to Victoria. The Japanese used for the most part light artillery and the firing was sporadic. The annoying thing was that although the guns were in full view, with their muzzle flashes clearly visible, nothing was available with which to retaliate. The large 9-inch coastal defence guns spread around the island all pointed out to sea and could not be brought to bear on the mainland. The reason for the comparatively light shelling became clear a couple of days later when suddenly all shelling stopped and an ominous silence broke out. Shortly after the artillery fell silent a small motor boat put out from Kowloon flying a large white flag. It contained two very smartly dressed, white-gloved Japanese army officers and proceeded at a leisurely pace across the harbour to Victoria. The two officers came ashore at a

61

spot near where the Mandarin Hotel stands today and were escorted to Government House. About half an hour later they returned to their launch and proceeded back across the harbour still flying the white flag. Within minutes of their reaching Kowloon the Japanese artillery opened up again, this time with far greater intensity. We learned later that the white flag party had delivered an ultimatum to the Governor demanding the surrender of Hong Kong Island. He was informed that failure to do so would result in the Colony being crushed under the feet of the Imperial Japanese Army with consequential heavy loss of life. The Governor instructed the plenipotentiaries to inform their masters that he rejected the ultimatum and sent them on their way.

Following this exchange it soon became apparent that the Japanese were making preparations to invade the island and one night some four days after the delivery of the ultimatum they made their first attempt. Swimmers were discovered trying to come ashore in the area of Causeway Bay. They were quickly repulsed but the build-up of small craft along the Kowloon waterfront, particularly around the Star Ferry piers, indicated that a major effort was about to be made. Without artillery the defenders could do little but watch developments, although one destroyer, HMS *Thracian*, was available. She was ordered to proceed from Aberdeen via the East Lama Channel to Victoria harbour and shell the concentration of boats around the piers on the Kowloon side. The attempt was made at night but on her way into harbour she ran aground off Stonecutters Island and had to limp back to Aberdeen. There she was put into dry dock to effect repairs but air attacks caused further damage and she was still in the dock at the time of the surrender. (I never did discover why she went aground. Perhaps she was staying too close to the shore in order to steer clear of the minefield we had laid and was therefore in unfamiliar waters. Hitherto, like all shipping in those days, she had had to enter and leave harbour through the Tathong Channel and the boom defence "gate" at Lei Mun. To the best of my knowledge *Thracian* had never previously entered harbour from the west.)

With the *Thracian* out of action (and now the principle target of the Japanese Air Force which repeatedly bombed her as she lay in the Aberdeen dry dock) the MTBs were sent in. They came roaring into the harbour at full throttle with their twin machine guns hammering away, dropped their torpedoes, turned around and raced back out to load their second set before dashing back in for another run. It was a brave effort that cost them dearly, particularly as torpedoes are not very effective against land targets. Those that did hit the piers did little damage, whereas three MTBs were sunk and others suffered hits from the hail of fire put up by the Japanese gunners. A few survivors managed to swim to the island and one or two others to Kowloon where they were taken prisoner.

With the naval effort spent it was rumoured that attempts were being made to realign one or more of the coastal gun batteries so that they could fire on the Japanese small-boat armada that was rapidly growing along the Kowloon quays and piers. As far as I am aware, however, such realignment was never achieved and we, who were by now holed up in the naval dockyard running from cover to cover whenever it was necessary to move, could only wait for the inevitable assault. We knew it would probably come in the early hours of the morning — the only question was where. It seemed to me that the naval dockyard was as good a place as any, the Japanese artillery had heavily pounded it and some accurately placed shells had destroyed the pillboxes on the mole. If they could take it the Japanese would have an excellent protected area in which to unload their heavy equipment, and would be within a stone's throw of Government House. In the event, and probably fortunately for me, the Japanese commander did not share my strategic thinking. The attack, when it came in the early hours of 18 December, was across the narrowest part of the Lei Yue Mun Channel in the area of the Taikoo docks and its adjacent power station.

As far as I could ascertain from survivors with whom I talked in the prison camps, it had not been considered likely by the British command that the invasion would be in that area. There were obviously insufficient troops to cover all the islands miles of shoreline so mobile task forces had been set up which could respond rapidly to any signs of attack. In the event the Japanese assault troops swam ashore and established a shallow beachhead before a small mobile unit of the 2nd Battalion of the Middlesex Regiment reached the landing point. When it did, it failed to push the invaders back into the sea and was overrun as fresh waves of assault troops landed from the armada of boats that had been assembled in Kowloon. The Japanese met the most stubborn resistance at the power station, which was defended by a group of the Hong Kong Volunteer Force consisting largely of elderly men, many of whom were in their sixties. Armed with nothing more than First World War Lee Enfield rifles and one light machine gun, they kept the invaders at bay for nearly twenty-four hours before, with all their ammunition exhausted, they were overrun.

Having established a base the invading force moved rapidly in the general direction of Stanley village, thus cutting the island in two. To support the hard-pressed Canadians the majority of the *Thracian's* crew (it being considered impossible to repair the ship under current circumstances) were despatched from Aberdeen in two lorries. At that point the speed of the Japanese advance had not been appreciated and it was not realized that they were already in the Violet Hill area. This lack of up-to-date intelligence proved fatal — the sailors were ambushed and mown down as they approached the Wong Nei Chong Gap. There were only six survivors, one or two of whom had been shot and left for dead.

Having split the island in two the Japanese deployed half of their forces to attack the fortified Stanley peninsular and the other half to attack in the direction of Victoria. The battle for Stanley was ferocious, the narrow approach being well defended with pillboxes and hastily dug trenches. The 2nd Middlesex defended their home base tenaciously as the Japanese attacked in human waves. The battle lasted four days with the invaders having to withdraw and regroup twice, but in the end sheer weight of numbers prevailed and by the time of the surrender only one defence line remained intact.

On the other end of the island the Japanese entered Causeway Bay and Happy Valley. At this point the dozen or so Royal Marines attached to the base ship HMS *Tamar* were despatched to assist the Canadians and Royal Scots who were endeavouring to stem the attack. We were instructed to destroy all code and cipher books, which we did by burning them in a huge bonfire, and to destroy the Codex and Cipherx machines. By this time electrical power had been cut off and we had some difficulty destroying the machines, even with pick axes and hammers. The small drums gave us the most trouble and we resorted to using blow torches on them and then hammering them to pieces, all of which were gathered up and thrown into the sea during the night. On Christmas Eve all us shipless sailors who had ended up in the dockyard were issued Lee Enfield rifles (just out of store and still covered with grease), a bandolier of ammunition and assembled to march to the front which at that time was thought to be in the area of the Naval Hospital. Just as we were about to leave the orders were changed — we were to blow up the gates of the graving dock and stay and defend the dockyard. The dock gates were demolished and the night was spent in sandbagged emplacements waiting for the enemy to arrive. They failed to appear and Christmas morning passed without any sign of them but in mid afternoon an officer came out to us and told us to lay down our arms — the Governor had signed an instrument of surrender.[4] It was not a very Merry Christmas Day. It was only later that we learned that the reason the Governor had decided to surrender was because the Japanese, having reached the middle of the island where the principal reservoirs were located, had turned off the whole of the water supply to Victoria, the island's largest city. Apparently the town had been without water for two or three days causing hardship to the civilian population and raising the possibility of various epidemics.

That night, as we pondered what the morrow would bring, the remaining operational MTBs left Aberdeen carrying the senior army Intelligence officer, two Chinese admirals and other VIPs.[5] Most of their crews, with the exception of the coxswains, were left behind with the rest of us.

Notes:

1. HMS *Thanet* reached Singapore and became part of the Singapore Local Defence Force defending the Singapore naval base. The official report as to what happened to her there reads as follows:

   Lt Cdr B.S. Davies' old WWI destroyer HMS *Thanet* and Lt Cdr W.T.A. Moran's HMAS *Vampire* are dispatched to make a night attack on troop transports at Endau about 80 miles North of Singapore. At 2037, approaching Endau, they engage a warship they take to be a destroyer, but actually is minesweeper W-1. *Vampire* launches two torpedoes at W-1, but

67

they miss. W-1 raises the alarm and the Allied destroyers continue towards Endau. At 0318 *Vampire* sights *Shirayuki* to port and launches two torpedoes at her, but they miss. Then *Thanet* launches all four of her torpedoes, but also misses. Both Allied destroyers open fire with their 4-inch guns. *Sendal* and *Shirayuki* (Japanese destroyers) return fire. The Allied destroyers retire SE at maximum speed.

At about 0400, the *Thanet* is hit in the engine and boiler rooms. Her speed falls off and an explosion wrecks the old destroyer. She goes dead in the water, lists heavily to starboard and begins to sink. *Vampire* lays a smoke screen, but *Thanet* is attacked by *Fubuki*, *Hatsuyuki*, *Amagiri*, *Yugiri* (Japanese destroyers) and W-1. At 0415 HMS *Thanet* sinks. *Vampire* is undamaged and without casualties, but she has no chance to pick up survivors. She makes for Singapore arriving there at 1000.

Troop transports *Kansai Maru* and *Kanbera Maru* are damaged in the action. Later *Shirayuki* picks up 31 survivors from HMS *Thanet*. They are never seen again.

Unofficial reports claim that some *Thanet* survivors managed to reach the shore either by swimming or on Carley floats and other pieces of wreckage It is said that they were seen making their way through the jungle to Singapore. Another report states that two RAF officers met up with a number of the *Thanet*'s crew south of the Mersing river, a boat was found and by rowing at night and sleeping during the day they made their way down the coast of

Malaya until they were picked up by a small thousand-ton coaster which took them on to Singapore.

The wreck of the *Thanet* has been found lying some twenty metres down in the area east of Port Kaban on Malaya's east coast. Apparently the bow section had broken away as she sank and now lies some distance from the main part of the wreck. She has become a favorite target for "sports divers".

2. HMS *Scout* returned to England and survived the war. She was broken up in 1946.

3. HMS *Thracian* was salvaged by the Japanese and named Patrol Boat No. 101 (1942) and later as Training Boat No. 1 (1944). She survived the war and was recaptured in Tokyo in 1945. She was scrapped in 1946.

4. It was not until many years after the war that I learned how the Governor contacted the Japanese military and arranged for the surrender of the Colony. The story was published in the *South China Morning Post* on the fiftieth anniversary of the end of the war. It had been recorded by one of the officers involved who, although he did not survive the captivity, had passed his report to a fellow officer who did.

The officer involved was Lieutenant Colonel H. Stewart (affectionately known to his men of the Middlesex Regiment as "Monkey Stewart"). When the Governor, having received General Maltby's advice that further resistance was not possible, decided to surrender the Colony, the question was how best to make contact with the Japanese commander. It was decided that Colonel Stewart and Group Captain H.T. Bennett, a Japanese linguist and senior intelligence officer, together with a corporal carrying a large white flag, should proceed to the Wanchai area where the front line appeared to be and attempt to make contact with or get a message to the Japanese High Command. They duly walked in the middle of the road and reached the vicinity of the China Fleet Club before being stopped by a group of Japanese soldiers. From there they were taken to what was probably a forward command post where the Japanese Lieutenant in charge, to whom they explained the reason for their visit, obviously did not know what to do with them. So he gave them tea and sent a message to higher authority. Some twenty minutes passed before two senior Japanese officers arrived and Bennet explained again why they were there. After some discussion between the Japanese and a number of telephone calls, the British delegation were told that the Japanese C-in-C would only discuss the question of surrender with the Governor of the Colony and the British C-in-C; fighting would continue until these persons joined the delegation and were taken to meet the General commanding the Japanese forces. One member of the British group was sent back to Government House to convey this message to Governor Mark Young and General Maltby who reluctantly made their way to Wanchai to join the delegation. The Japanese then took them across the harbour to

Kowloon and the Peninsular Hotel, which the Japanese were using as their headquarters. They met the Japanese commander, Lieutenant General Sakai, who presented the formal surrender documents which Governor Young had no option but to sign late on Christmas Day. It was a candlelit surrender because electric power had been cut off and the only light available in the hotel was provided by candles.

The signing of the documents was the signal for the Japanese Command to grant its troops a three-day "no discipline" reward. From Boxing Day until 28 December, Japanese troops ran riot in Hong Kong. They plundered, killed and raped at will, displaying all the bestial characteristics they had previously shown during their war with China. It is estimated that over 10,000 women of all ages were raped by Japanese troops during that three-day period, referred to by some as the "Sacking of Hong Kong".

They had shown similar behaviour during the battle, during which they killed most of the prisoners they took, either by bayoneting or beheading, whilst hostilities were in progress. They bombed and shelled hospitals, completely destroying the Canossian Hospital on Peak Road and badly damaging the Matilda Hospital on the Peak. Both the Military Hospital on Bowen Road and the Naval Hospital on the Wanchai/Causeway Bay border were heavily shelled.

When they overran other places being used as temporary hospitals they often massacred the inmates. The most infamous and well-researched incident took place at St Stephen's College on the Stanley peninsular. When they entered the college the Japanese ordered everybody out and promptly shot four doctors who said that it was not possible to move the badly wounded. The Japanese then proceeded to bayonet the wounded as they lay in bed and when they had killed them all, together with some male orderlies, they turned their attention on the nurses. They took them into a small room and repeatedly raped them before killing them and mutilating their bodies. Seven nurses died this way and it is believed that fifty-six soldiers were bayoneted and killed as they lay in their hospital beds.

5. A number of accounts of what happened on that Christmas Day have been written by escapees and by historians. They vary marginally but it seems that five MTBs were still serviceable at the time of the surrender. The British commander, Major General Maltby, having agreed to aid the escape of a Chinese admiral and his staff (the Admiral and one of his senior aides had a Japanese price on their heads), sent instructions on Christmas morning that he and his group should proceed to the Naval establishment at Aberdeen, there to meet up with a group of senior British officers who were also attempting to escape. When the Admiral arrived the MTBs had already left so he and his followers commandeered a motorboat and escaped to one of the nearby islands under machine-gun fire from the Japanese. Fortunately for the Admiral, one of the MTBs came back during the night looking for him. He was picked up, the boat joined the other

four and proceeded at his suggestion to an island in Mirs Bay on the Colony's northern border. There he had contacts who advised the escapees to cross to the mainland, remove all equipment from the boats and scuttle them. This was done and the group was lead by friendly communist guerillas through Japanese-held territory to the nearest Nationalist stronghold at a place named Huizhou. They arrived there on 29 December. It is claimed that sixty-two British officers, which included the Intelligence and Information officers, were in the group that escaped and some of them got back to England about ten months after they left Hong Kong.

CHAPTER
FIVE

On Becoming a POW

In the early days of the Pacific War the Japanese armies swept across South-East Asia creating their so called "Co-prosperity Sphere". Whenever they captured large numbers of prisoners they sent them on long and punishing route marches, the object of which was, I suppose, to display the fallen masters to the local population, thus ensuring loss of face and to punish those who had the temerity to resist the army of the sun god, Hirohito. It might also have been done with a view to eliminating the sick and the frail, thousands of whom died on some of the more brutal marches. As Hong Kong was the first major base to fall the Japanese commander had no precedent to guide him. As a result, although he followed the predetermined course of action, the route march we were forced to take was nothing like as bad as some that took place later in other parts of South-East Asia. (The infamous Bataan march in the Philippines was probably the worst. There the surviving defenders of the Bataan Peninsular in Manila Bay were marched to a camp 85 miles north for no reason other than sheer vindictiveness. Thousands of American and Philippino troops died on the march from exhaustion or by being shot because they could not keep up.)

Ours began on 27 December when hordes of Japanese troops entered the dockyard and began moving us across the road to the Murray Road barracks. When we got there we found it had already been ransacked and almost everything movable had been taken. We were told to find blankets and mess kits (not that there was any food available), and be prepared to move on the next day. I never did find a mess kit but I did manage to locate a blanket, a 9-inch shallow pie dish, a spoon and what had once been a canvas cutlery holder, all of which served me in good stead over the following months. During the long night spent on the floor in the Murray Road barracks the possibility of escape was endlessly discussed as it had been since the time of the surrender. Regrettably no one could come up with a scheme that had even a possibility of success. There were three major drawbacks. Firstly, even if we could steal a boat and avoid all Japanese naval patrols, the Japs occupied all the surrounding land areas. Secondly, we were too big and had the wrong coloured skin; we would stand out like a sore thumb in a crowd of Orientals. Thirdly, none of us could speak Cantonese or Mandarin. Few slept much that night and in the morning the Japs started rounding us up firstly to count us, a somewhat lengthy process, and then to herd us through the gates en route for the Star Ferry. On the way we passed the Hong Kong Club cricket ground in Central Victoria and here I witnessed the ultimate act of sacrilege. On that immaculate piece of greensward, arguably one of the finest cricket pitches outside the United Kingdom, the Japs had parked all the cars, trucks and vans they could find and had commandeered. We were obviously in the hands of barbarians and events over the next few years were to prove the accuracy of that assessment.

Once past the cricket ground we were herded slowly along to the Star Ferry pier and literally crammed on board an already grossly overcrowded ferry boat, which proceeded straight across the harbour to the pier where the *Man Yeung* had docked the night of the search for stragglers. After disembarking we were counted again and apparently there must have been a discrepancy for to the accompaniment of much shouting and sword waving by the little martinet who appeared to be in charge, we were counted three more times. When at last the headman was satisfied he marched off, leaving us, and I am equally sure the guards, wondering what was to happen next. The latter milled around talking to each other and looking as fed up as I felt. They relieved their boredom by castigating any prisoner who sat down or stepped out of line. An hour passed before another Jap officer appeared. He wore a light green coloured uniform whereas all the rest were in drab khaki and we soon discovered that he was the official interpreter having learnt his English as a porter in a Canadian hotel. What I presumed to be the NCOs gathered round the newcomer and when they broke up returned to their troops shouting instructions and gesticulating that we were to get on the move. The troops emphasized the point with the liberal use of rifle buts and copious face slapping. So we moved on past the YMCA and the Peninsular Hotel, and for a while I thought we were headed for the railway station to be shipped off to some godforsaken place in the middle of China. This fear passed, however, when I could see that the head of the column of prisoners had turned left up Nathan Road. When I eventually got there I found that both sides of the street were lined with Chinese waving Japanese flags and all the windows above street level were crowded with people doing the same thing. I wondered how they came by the flags so quickly; had they been making them ever since the Japanese invaded? They were waving them enthusiastically but there did not appear to be much joy in their faces, in fact some looked downright sad and I noticed one or two who seemed to be crying. Then I noticed that in addition to the guards who were prodding us along there were Japanese soldiers moving behind the crowds on the pavement and it dawned on me that I was witnessing a propaganda exercise. No wonder the flags were all the same — they had been handed out by the Japs with instructions to wave them or else!

Somehow this realization seemed to help. We were not like the slaves brought back to a cheering Rome by a victorious general; the crowds here were in many ways worse off than we were. Hong Kong's civilian population suffered badly during the occupation. It was exposed not only to all the excesses of a brutal occupying force, but also to the cruelties of the criminal gangs (called Triads) which cooperated with the Japanese. As we moved on up Nathan Road some of the chaps who were lugging mattresses and heavy kit bags began to weaken and stopped to take a breather. They were immediately jumped on by the guards who prodded them with bayonets, hit them round the head with rifle buts and forced them to keep moving, usually leaving their heavy baggage on the road. We were kept moving up Nathan Road, past the intersection with Waterloo Road, into what was unfamiliar territory for me, and then a very welcome halt was called. With all the benefits of hindsight the halt was probably not called in order to give us a rest, but because at that point many of the officers were separated from the troops and marched off towards a camp in Argyle Street. The rest of us were forced on up Nathan Road until we approached what at that time were the outskirts of the city. Then the column turned sharply left into the Sham Shui Po district and there, totally gutted, was an old army barracks into which we were directed. I estimated that we had marched some 3 to 3½ miles, even though it felt like 33 in the state we were in. Little did we realize how fortunate we were. By the standard of subsequent marches we might have been sent all round the New Territories.

If Murray Road barracks had been ransacked, Sham Shui Po barracks had been denuded. The camp comprised lines of substantial rectangular huts built of composition blocks on a concrete base. At the seaward end there was a three-storied brick-built building known as Jubilee Buildings, which had been the married quarters. In peacetime, no doubt these facilities provided reasonable accommodation. There was running water, electric light and ceiling fans, but by the time we arrived all this had gone. The doors, door frames, windows, window frames, ceiling tiles, ceiling fans, light fittings and light switches had all been removed — all that was left were the bare concrete floor, the walls, the roof trusses and the roof. This was our new home.

Fortunately, although we had been separated from most of the officers there remained with us that excellent brand of middle management that all services possess to a greater or lesser degree — the non-commissioned officer. They certainly proved their worth in those early days in Sham Shui Po. They took stock of the situation, equitably divided the accommodation, organized fair distribution of what little food there was and more important, stood between us and the face-slapping guards and interpreters. "God", the Regulating Chief Petty Officer who had ruled us in peacetime was now our spokesperson with the Japs, and his vigorous efforts to improve our lot cost him dearly. Sometimes he would be set upon by two bow-legged Japanese soldiers whose heads were level with his massive chest and they would jump up as they punched him in the face. They would rain blow after blow on him in their efforts to knock him over but they never succeeded. He was a better man than his diminutive Japanese tormentors and to their great chagrin all they managed to force from him was a look of utter contempt. (He was not the only tall person to whom the Japanese took exception — they seemed to have a grudge against anyone who could look down on them. It was for this reason that the tall, lanky Canadians suffered so badly at the hands of the Japanese.) Nevertheless, as a result of his efforts and of others like him a sort of routine was established which would have been difficult to achieve without a degree of service discipline. Even in the Hong Kong Volunteer Defence Force lines this discipline prevailed, although some of the privates in peacetime had been the taipans and the NCOs ex-servicemen employed as instructors. There was however, one difference between that group and the rest of us. Some of them had relatives in the city (for there were a number of Chinese among them) and others had very loyal Chinese servants. These people would come to the far side of the street on the south side of the camp (they were not allowed near the wire) in the hope of gaining news of their relatives or employers. If they saw somebody they knew they would endeavour to communicate with them by shouting across the street until the guards stopped them. On one such occasion a young Chinese lady carrying a small baby came to that street and desperately tried to shout a message to one of the prisoners in the camp. A guard yelled at her and whilst she was still calling grabbed the baby, threw it at another guard who caught it on his bayonet and threw it on to a third guard who did the same. They kept this up for a few minutes before throwing the lifeless child back to its mother. Instinctively she caught the bloody bundle and was driven off by the guards.

Barbarism such as this increased our hatred of the Japs and led to more discussion as to the possibility of escape. At that time the camp had the sea at one end and on one side. On the other side was the street with buildings the whole length but the fourth side (the one opposite Jubilee Buildings) was an open field from which we were separated by a hastily erected barbed-wire fence. We could see clearly across open ground to the Lion Rock and watched daily as columns of Chinese, their possessions on their backs, were driven along the road that borders Beacon Hill and so out of Hong Kong. What happened to them I do not know but I imagine it was not a pleasant fate. Whilst watching them we noticed that there were two guards outside the wire on that side of the camp who were changed every hour. A sergeant would march the replacements to the centre point, relieve the guards and march the retiring pair back to the guard house which was on the street side of the camp. The new guards would turn 90 degrees, one left and one right and march to the end of the fence. There they would about turn and strut back to the centre, the time interval between leaving each other en route for the end of the fence and meeting again in the middle being exactly eleven minutes. Given a dark moonless night that interval was considered long enough to crawl under the wire and get well into the decaying vegetation that covered the field before the guards turned. With that realization, and spurred by the atrocities we had witnessed, escape plans were again seriously discussed. Of the three obstacles that had deterred us before, we had managed to overcome one. We had befriended a young Cantonese-speaking Chinese from the HKVDF and he agreed to come with us. There remained, however, the problem of Japanese control of the mainland, and the need to acquire a map and some food to take with us. We were working on this with reasonable hope of success when fate played another card — all naval personnel were ordered to be transferred to a camp at North Point within twenty-four hours. So the escape attempt was never made by us, but I have reason to believe that our Chinese friend and one other did make the attempt and succeeded.

As soon as it was learned that we were to be moved, we anticipated another route march, but this did not happen for a Star Ferry boat appeared at the Jubilee Buildings quayside and we were counted aboard. Once we were embarked and a new set of guards was satisfied that they had the right number of prisoners, the ferry set off in the direction of North Point. We were about halfway there when another ferry, going in the opposite direction, passed us. It too was loaded with prisoners of war but they were all army types. On arrival we were counted again and released into a pretty squalid camp comprising a number of wooden huts and millions of flies. I had never seen so many flies in all my life and no matter what we did to try to get rid of them we failed to reduce their number so that they remained a threat and added to the general misery throughout our stay at North Point. They were undoubtedly a factor in the wave of dysentery that broke out and which claimed as its first victim one of the last and certainly the youngest Coder to be sent to Hong Kong just before the Far East war started. Whilst we were at North Point in

February 1942, a military hospital still existed at Bowen Road. It functioned under extreme difficulty but function it did and somehow permission was obtained to take our sick shipmate there. As he was carried out head first on a stretcher, with a swarm of flies on and around his face, he made no move to brush them off. The next day news was received that he had died. (He is now buried with other naval personnel in the military cemetery at Stanley). This event made us realize how vulnerable we were and that disease rather than the Japs was now perhaps our greatest enemy. The death of one of our own undoubtedly depressed us, but another event at North Point was soon to elate us. When we arrived at North Point we found that there were still some Army personnel in residence, including a few junior officers. Although I knew nothing about it at the time they had been making plans for an escape, but like the little group of my close friends they were without fluency in the local languages. Our arrival apparently brought at least two people who could rectify that deficiency, for among the naval ratings captured in Hong Kong was the boom defence crew. I had not met these people but they comprised ratings who had retired from the Navy having served their twenty-one years and had been called back at the outbreak of war in September 1939. Among them were two chaps in their mid-forties who had taken their retirement discharge in Shanghai and had joined the Police Force there. Both had married, one to a white Russian and the other to a Chinese lady. Both apparently were fluent in Mandarin and the one with the Chinese wife could not only also speak fluent Cantonese but also had some ability in the languages spoken in northern China. Unbeknown to us, he must somehow have been discovered and approached by the Army escape committee, who asked if he would be prepared to join an overland escape attempt. As we were now back on Hong Kong Island he must have asked how they were intending to get to the mainland to start the overland attempt. A solution to that problem had already been found. Chinese friends on the outside had been contacted and on a night with no moon, and when the tides were due to rise to exceptionally high levels, with the incoming current sweeping along the sides of the camp, they would arrange for an empty sampan to drift right up to the camp fence. The first intimation that I or any of my friends had that anything unusual was happening was when a couple of Army types came into our hut and requested that we attend a sing-song to be held at eight o'clock that evening in one of the huts on the other side of the camp, nearest to the road. Furthermore, he asked if we would make a hell of a lot of noise around lights out (10.00 pm), and keep singing until the Japs came round to stop the noise and drive us back to our own huts. I do not think any of us felt like singing but we performed as requested and were duly chased back to our own huts by furious guards swinging their rifles at us with great gusto and shouting what were doubtless gross obscenities, but sounded, as did most of their verbal communications, like the noise one hears when pigs are being driven into an abattoir.

The escape was not discovered until the next morning's roll call and then all hell broke out. Japanese officers harangued the sergeants who did the same to the troops who took it out on us. They slapped faces indiscriminately and hit people around the head with their rifle buts. Again the chief petty officers bore the brunt of this display of bad temper. We were kept standing on the parade ground for over three hours and before we were released the Camp Commandant made a blistering speech in which he complained that we had shown great ingratitude for all he had tried to do for our welfare! He then announced that until further notice rations would be cut by 50 per cent.

When we were back in our huts we were told the full story of the night's events. The "after hours" part of the sing-song had, as anticipated, diverted the Jap guards away from the fence on the seaward side. An empty sampan had successfully been floated alongside and three people, including our chap from the boom defence crew, had escaped. Furthermore, they had taken with them, wrapped in oilskin, a list containing the names, rank and serial numbers of every prisoner in the camp. This news was certainly a boost for morale and everybody prayed that the three escapees would make it home. (We of course heard nothing further of them but they did make it home and fairly quickly at that. When I got home in the autumn of 1945 my mother told me that in August 1942 she had received a telegram from the Admiralty informing her that her son was alive and a prisoner of war in enemy hands. There was no way the Admiralty could have known this unless our escapees had succeeded. When I passed through a transit camp in Manila on my way home I met some survivors of the boom defence crew who had been kept in the Sham Shui Po camp throughout the war. They told me that the Able Seaman who had escaped from North Point in 1942 returned to Hong Kong in the first Royal Navy vessel to enter harbour at the end of the war — but as a Lieutenant Commander. If anyone deserved the promotion he certainly did.)

Not long after the escape, and possibly as a result of it, we were shipped back to Sham Shui Po. There we found that security had been tightened and a high-voltage electric fence now surrounded the camp. The Japanese were obviously trying to ensure that there were no more escapes. Shortly after our return they ordered everybody onto the parade ground and demanded that we all sign a pledge not to escape. The few remaining Army officers who helped administer the camp refused to sign and they spoke for all the rest of us. (What the Japanese were demanding contravened the Geneva Convention but as the Japs had not signed that Convention it did not worry them.) So we stood for hours on the parade ground with machine guns aimed at us wishing the Japs to hell. After nearly five hours of stand-off the Army officers decided that further delay was causing severe suffering among the sick and the elderly (there were a number of Merchant Navy captains in the camp, most of whom were in their late sixties) and decided to sign under duress on behalf of the whole camp. This done the Japs had everybody listed in groups of five and announced that henceforth should anyone escape or try to escape, the other members of his quintet would be executed. These moves did not of themselves prevent any further attempts at escape. What did prevent them was the sharp decline in health and physical strength resulting from what was by now nearly six mouths of living on a starvation diet.

CHAPTER
SIX

On Mice and Men and Malnutrition

The daily food ration provided by the Japs in Sham Shui Po camp was one small bowl of rice in the morning and one at night. In addition, a bowl of very watery unsalted soup made from unidentifiable vegetation was provided at the evening meal. The rice was full of mice droppings and a few tiny beetle-like insects, and was recognized by those that knew of these things as the sweepings from the godown floors. The vegetation was less readily identified by either the Caucasian or the Oriental inmates. In the view of the few Army doctors who had been left with the troops, the diet was insufficient to maintain life over the long term. By June 1942 it began to look as though they could be right.

We began to feel very lethargic — it was almost too much trouble to move. The shape of one's body began to change as ribs showed up in the chest, thigh and calf muscles began to contract, and hip and leg bones became discernible. A painful phenomena which for the want of a better word was termed "electric feet" swept through the camp. It comprised sharp stabbing pains in the feet that were particularly bad at night, making it almost impossible to get to sleep. Then it seemed our bodies began to decay as the corners of ones mouth cracked open and unsightly sores formed which became magnets for the hordes of flies that permeated the camp. Inside the mouth long, narrow, yellow blisters appeared, whilst in the centre of the ball of the foot a deep yellow "concave" blister formed that made the simple act of walking painful. The scrotum began to itch intolerably, turned red and became sticky. In some cases the scrotum became infected and swelled up with septicaemia. When that happened, there being no medicines with which to treat the condition (the Japs adamantly refused to supply any even though it was known that there were ample medical supplies in Hong Kong), the poor chap inevitably died.

By this time we were getting used to people dying. As at North Point amoebic dysentery was rampant and was taking its toll, particularly among the young. The Royal Scots lost many of their young soldiers to this painful, debilitating disease. Every effort was made under the direction of the Army medical officers to keep the camp clean and the flies under control and this undoubtedly helped to contain the dysentery problem, but it proved impossible to eliminate it. This in part at least was due to the fact that the camp had only one central cookhouse. We had to go there to collect our ration of rice in whatever utensil we had and then take it back to the hut to eat it. This involved walking nearly a quarter of a mile with the food exposed to attack by disease-carrying flies. I remembered what my father had told me about a similar problem in the camps on India's North-West Frontier and followed his example. As soon as I received my rice ration I covered my plate with the canvas utensil holder I had picked up in the Murray Road barracks. Whereas many around me contracted dysentery and some died from it, I did not. Probably that was sheer luck but I like to think that the canvas cover had something to do with it.

In July and August 1942, a new and even more deadly disease struck — diphtheria. In normal circumstances an outbreak of diphtheria is rapidly contained by a program of inoculation and the use of anti-diphtheria serum. It was known that ample supplies of the medications necessary to contain the outbreak and eradicate the disease from the camp were in the military and civilian hospitals in the Colony. But these were not normal circumstances and despite urgent pleas by the doctors, the Japanese general who was the acting Governor of Hong Kong refused to permit any of these supplies to be brought into the camp.

Accordingly, in my judgment, the Japanese general and the sadistic Camp Commandant, Colonel Tokunaga, were guilty of premeditated murder, for they knew that without the medications two out of every three who contracted the disease would die — and such was indeed the case. With potassium permanganate gargles as the only treatment available, there was little our medical people could do to stem the tide and the number of deaths rapidly mounted. A large lorry piled high with the coffins of those who had died during the night left the camp every morning.[1] All those who contracted the disease were moved to isolation huts around which a barrier was erected to prevent anyone coming too close. Every evening, after roll call, a list of those not expected to survive the night was posted, and in July, unbeknown to me at the time, my name was on that list on three consecutive days. It had started as a sore throat and on admitting it to a medical orderly I was whisked into the isolation area where it was confirmed that I had contracted diphtheria. I was laid on a blanket on the floor of the hut and twice a day given potassium permanganate solution with which to gargle. The only utensil I possessed that was capable of holding liquid was an old coffee tin, so the purple liquid was poured into it and another somewhat larger tin was brought around in which one disposed of the stuff — not the ideal treatment for diphtheria and I did not thrive on it. I just lay there and apparently, although I did not know it, the medics thought I was dying. Then, in the middle of the night when I was not feeling at all well, an Army doctor came in shining a flashlight on the faces of the figures on the ground. He stopped and stooped over the body of the chap lying next to me, a lieutenant in the Royal Army Service Corps, and I saw that whilst he held a flashlight in one hand, in the other was a hypodermic syringe. He exposed the Lieutenant's arm, rubbed it with a piece of what looked like cotton wool and then inserted the needle into the arm. He began to push the plunger of the syringe and then stopped and put his hand on the sick man's neck. Then he withdrew his hand, fished a stethoscope out of his pocket and listened to the man's heart. He stood up, stepped over the Lieutenant, knelt down by me and said, "Here, old chap, there are only a few cc's left but they might do you a bit of good," whereupon he plunged the needle in my arm and emptied the remaining contents of the syringe into it. What he injected was diphtheria serum and it undoubtedly saved my life. I began to recover and ere long was moved out of the critically ill hut, where one was taken to die, into an adjacent hut where — luxury of luxuries — my blankets were laid on top of an iron cot (in many ways it was less comfortable than the floor but I thought I was going up in the world). Eighteen years were to pass before I learned that the diphtheria serum that had saved my life had been smuggled into Sham Shui Po by a Japanese interpreter who was a devout Christian. When his activity was discovered he was severely punished and he was transferred to an island in the Dutch East Indies. Although he survived the war he found on his return to his native Tokyo that all his family had been killed in air raids.

It took a very long time to recover from the bout of diphtheria and whilst I was still in what I suppose might have been termed the recovery hut, it was rumoured that all Navy personnel were to be moved. The Church of England padre, who regularly visited the sick and spoke to every patient in the huts, first broke the news to me. He had been the naval padre attached to HMS *Tamar* and he confided in me that it was thought that naval personnel would comprise a large part of a contingent of prisoners of war that was to be shipped off to Japan. An army Roman Catholic padre also visited the sick periodically and as it happened he came in a couple of days after his naval colleague first told me of the rumour. So through one of my fellow patients I endeavoured to discover whether he could confirm it (I had to ask through another patient because this particular padre would speak only to Catholics and ignored everybody else), but he was non-committal. However, my friends used to come down to the isolation huts most evenings and although a barrier kept them from getting too close, once I was moved to the recovery hut they could see me through the holes where the windows used to be and would shout words of encouragement. It was they who confirmed the move a week or so later. They had been warned to be ready to move at twenty-four hours' notice and they would be allowed to take very little with them. About four days after that they came to say goodbye as they were leaving the following morning.[2] I wished them good luck and when they turned away was overcome with a feeling of loneliness and self-pity for I had spent the last two years in their company. They had been my constant companions with whom I had shared all the joys, the dangers and the miseries of that turbulent time and now it seemed I was to be left very much on my own.

Of course, I was not really on my own for I was surrounded by people, and a lot of them were in worse condition than I was. So the melancholy mood soon passed, assisted in no small measure by the cheerful repartee that constantly flowed between the long-suffering medical orderlies and the patients. The latter talked between themselves mainly of the past and sometimes about what they would like to do after the war. We all indulged in a form of self-torture by talking about restaurants we used to know and our favourite meals. We visualized what we would have immediately if we could wave a magic wand and have it appear. I seem to recall that my order consisted of two things: my mother's roast pork with the crackling slightly burned, and a fresh baked cottage loaf with a pound of farmhouse butter. With these thoughts in mind I slowly recovered mobility. It was difficult at first because I had lain on my back for so long that the tendons at the back of my legs had shrunk, so that when I attempted to stand up the feet failed to bend up properly. For a while, until the tendons stretched, I had to walk with my legs wide apart, which attracted a lot of ribald comments. Gradually, though, I got back to normal and was discharged from the diphtheria huts.

I went back to what was left of the naval contingent. We were now down to less than forty men, all of whom like me had been sick at the time of the draft, or had been considered too old to travel. The latter included all that was left of the boom defence crew and we were all housed in one hut. It was here that I passed my second summer in Sham Shui Po and it was here in September 1943 that I contracted malaria. As usual there was no medication but there was something else — there was the boom defence crew. These rough diamonds divided themselves into four watches and for seventy-two hours continuously swabbed me down with wet pieces of any rags or cloth they could put their hands on. As a result the fever passed, I recovered and can never thank them enough. They were a tough bunch who although married with wives in England, all had a second Chinese "wife" in Hong Kong. With one exception they used some pretty colourful language. The exception, who had become a postman after leaving the Navy, had embraced religion and refused to swear. So whilst his contemporaries had no inhibitions as to their choice of words, when he was annoyed he confined his comments to "suffering beef rings". From where the expression came I have no idea but I do know that in later life I have often used it myself, and thought of the man and his friends who nursed me back to health. They were the salt of the earth and if I was in a tough spot ever again they, more than anyone else I can think of, are the ones I would wish to be with. It was not long after the bout of malaria that I was put on a draft to Japan. I did not see any of the boom defence chaps again until I met up with some of them in a camp near Manila in the Philippines on my way home. They had all survived and meeting them was almost like seeing my own family.

Notes:

1. Although the Japs in Hong Kong would not permit medication to be brought into Sham Shui Po camp, they were quite willing to provide coffins. All the prisoners who died in Hong Kong were buried. In

Japan, at the Narumi and Toyama camps, the military ordered cremation of all who died.

2. Some two months after they left a rumour circulated that the ship on which they were being taken to Japan had been sunk but it was not until after the war that I learned the full story. The ship, the *Lisbon Maru*, was torpedoed by an American submarine on 2 October 1942. Of the 1,816 POWs on board, only 977 survived and of these, as far as I have been able to ascertain, only one was from the Royal Navy signals group. He told me that the prisoners were packed like sardines at the very bottom of the ship's hold, from which the only way out was up a narrow vertical ladder. When the torpedo struck panic ensued and men tried to force their way on deck where they were promptly mown down by machine-gun fire from the Jap guards. The ship died slowly, remaining afloat for nearly four hours by which time rescue craft had arrived and the Japs decided to let the POWs up on deck. This provoked a stampede and men fell off the ladder on to the heads of those below, in at least one case breaking the neck of a man at the foot of the ladder. My informant was one of the last to climb out and he recalls seeing "God" and the Chief Supply Petty Officer sitting near the base of the ladder playing crib with a home-made pack of cards. They had no intention of leaving and went down with the ship, as did the Chief Yeomen of Signals who had welcomed me into his department when I first arrived in the Colony. With one exception — who like me had

been confined to a "hospital" hut when the draft left Sham Shui Po — all the friends who had helped me celebrate my twenty-first birthday perished when the ill-fated *Lisbon Maru* sank.

She was one of fifteen ships carrying POWs that are known to have been sunk in the Pacific area by Allied submarines and aircraft. A complete list will be found at the end of this book.

CHAPTER
SEVEN

On Travel

During 1943 other drafts of POWs had been sent off, presumably to Japan, and as the number of inmates fell, the size of the Sham Shui Po camp was reduced in October by moving the electric fence on the northern side some hundred yards closer to the Jubilee Buildings. We interpreted this move as an indication that "drafting" had come to an end as the supply of relatively fit prisoners had been exhausted. In November, however, a sports day was ordered, we were lined up in groups and forced to compete in "races". The nasty little green-uniformed Jap interpreter (the ex-Vancouver bell hop) strutted around shouting orders which were echoed by his poodle, the notorious Major Boon, the English officer appointed to liaise with the camp administrative staff, admittedly not an easy job but it seemed to most of us that he was more on the side of the Japs than ours. He helped the interpreter and the guards ensure that everyone took part in the "races", even if they had to be encouraged to the starting line by the prod of a bayonet or the bang on the head with a rifle butt. Suffering from beriberi and painful blisters on my feet, to say nothing of having just recovered from a bout of malaria, the best I could do was hobble up a few yards from the start line — which I thought was perhaps just as well when I noticed the Japs took the name and number of all those who managed to complete the 50-yard course. It did not seem to matter how long they took or whether they were limping or staggering as long as they finished the course. My suspicion was well founded for a week later another draft of 300 men was announced and all those whose names had been taken on the "sports day" were on it. Among them were six Navy personnel comprising the other ex-Shanghai policeman, one telegraphist, one seaman, two motor mechanic petty officers from the MTB flotilla and my friend Ken Shipsides, a RN sick bay attendant. They were included with forty-four members of the HK volunteers to make up a group of fifty.

They were given a water bottle and this, together with one blanket, was all they were told they could take with them. It grieved me to see them go, especially the sick berth attendant Ken Shipsides, who had been a tower of strength in the isolation hut where I had been put when I had diphtheria. Those of us who were left watched the preparations and wondered what would happen to us. The Japs were obviously scraping the barrel to make up the 300. Would their next move be the elimination of the remainder? In the event they did not do so, but two days before the draft's scheduled departure date they announced a list of "reserve or standby" prisoners, and my name was on it. At the time I was not sure what that meant but the old boys (they were all of forty-five!) of the boom defence crew who had nursed me through malaria assured me that I would not be taken because with beriberi and bad feet I could not get around very well. However, on the day of departure the draft was lined up in groups of fifty and the standby personnel in parties of ten facing the main groups. When the latter were counted, if they fell short of fifty because a nominee had died or was too sick to be moved, there was no immediate face-slapping inquiry as would normally be the case, but a replacement was immediately taken from the standby parties. When the combined HK volunteer/Royal Navy group was counted it came up two people short, so together with one other Navy seaman I was moved to join the draftees and we were marched off straight away to some waiting trucks that took us to the Kowloon docks. The move was over so quickly that I had no chance to say goodbye to those naval types remaining in Hong Kong.

When we reached the dock I was surprised to see that we were being herded on to a tiny coastal steamer about as long as a Star Ferry but narrower. I wondered how they were going to get 300 aboard, but soon found out. They kept ramming us down into the single hold with the liberal use of rifle butts, kicks and the usual cacophony of animal sounds, which seemed to be the hallmark of Nipponese soldiers enjoying themselves. Two small electric light bulbs at the top of the hold gave some illumination and we found that there was bamboo matting on the floor. There was not enough room, however, for everybody to lie down at the same time, so we divided ourselves into three groups — one would stand, one sit and one lie, with positions being changed every two hours. Of course there were no toilet provisions in the hold but by kind permission of the guards, prisoners were allowed on deck two at a time to make use of the splendid facilities specially built into the ship during its recent refit. And splendid they were indeed, copied directly from Columbus's original blueprint that comprised a timber platform protruding out from the stern which enabled two people to sit on a plank with a hole in it, with their derrières between 2 and 8 feet over the water depending on the wave height. Adjacent to this masterpiece of marine engineering, another contraption had been erected which comprised two large rice boilers perched on top of wood-burning stoves that had been especially installed so that this little coastal tramp steamer could fulfill its new and enhanced role as a prison ship. Unfortunately, whoever installed these ingenious pieces of equipment was obviously not familiar with the moods of the sea (or was it malice aforethought on the part of Chinese saboteurs?) and had not reckoned on the gale we ran into on our second night at sea. With one contemptuous wave the sea swept the whole lot over the side.

Our voyage had started the moment the last of us had been forced into the hold. As none were allowed on deck at that time we could not see what was happening or where we were headed, but when the ship began to pitch gently up and down we knew we were moving into open water. It was a beautiful sunny morning when we "embarked", and by the time it eventually became my turn to go up on deck it was late evening and the sun was setting on a calm and placid sea. We were well out of sight of land and as far as I could judge moving on a north-easterly course. The latrine arrangements, although primitive, did have one thing in their favour in that it gave one the opportunity to study, at close quarters, the ship's wake and to judge the speed that we were making. It seemed to me that the ship was just crawling along at some 5 to 6 knots, at which speed it was obviously going to take a long time to reach Japan if that was indeed our destination. Back in the hold, listening to the asthmatic cough of the engine and feeling its vibrations, coupled with those of the rumbling propeller shaft, I wondered whether the Jap skipper was deliberately going slow in order to run in his newly refurbished engines. When I ventured this suggestion wiser and more knowledgeable people said that it was not a matter of running in but rather one of running out. The engine sounded to them in bad shape and they thought it might pack up at any moment. With this cheerful thought in mind I spent the rest of the night waiting for it to happen, but it did not and the next morning it was still going, albeit sounding even more asthmatic. When I eventually got up on deck I noticed that the sky had clouded over and could see that the motion felt in the hold was caused by a strong swell that seemed to be crossing our bow. It was rendering the efforts of two cooks and their Japanese taskmasters difficult as they laboured with the wood stoves and rice boilers that were constantly moving through a 45-degree arc. Somehow, though, they managed to cook some rice and we had our first shipboard meal. As the day passed the motion of the ship became more pronounced, the wind rose and by nightfall we were in a full-blown gale. The little ship staggered on with its engine spluttering away and I sensed the captain had turned her into the wind for we were now experiencing a very strong pitching motion which made life very uncomfortable in the overcrowded hold. It became difficult to stand and men fell on top of others sitting or lying. The whole mass of us began to slide first one way and then the other, and although some people were badly bruised we were fortunate that no one was seriously injured that night. Morning brought relief, the storm abated and we were able to sort ourselves out, only to find that it had swept away the latrines and cooking facilities, and with them any hope we had of being fed that day. Whilst we were bemoaning this unfortunate fact we were suddenly hit by silence — the wretched engine had stopped and all we could hear was the slapping of the sea on the ship's hull and the water sloshing about in the bilges beneath our feet. These soft, sibilant sounds seemed to amplify the enormity of the silence occasioned by the withdrawal of the asthmatic thumping of the engine and the low-pitched rumble of the propeller shaft.

This untoward turn of events had obviously caught the attention of the Japs for they could be heard rushing about shouting in their own inimitable guttural form of communication. The shutdown was evidently not voluntary and it seemed that the little subjects of the Sun God were at panic stations. In one respect it pleased us to see them so, but on the other hand I cannot say that we felt too happy about the situation, for as we wallowed stationary in the by now gentle swell we were a sitting duck for any passing US submarine, and we remained that way until the evening. During the day the cooks had somehow managed to cook some rice and we had a tiny ration each, while temporary latrines comprising two large buckets that required frequent emptying were set up on the deck. Whilst a working party was attending to this chore in the late afternoon an aircraft flew over us and our chaps reported that it was a float plane bearing Japanese markings. An hour later to cheers of "Banzai" by the Japanese crew, the engine, after a couple of false starts, spluttered back into life and the little ship got under way again.

We sailed on into the night but on the following day around noon a very loud bang was heard coming from the direction of the engine room, and once more the ship lay dead in the water. We stayed that way for the rest of the day and the following night, during which the crew did not appear to be doing anything to rectify the problem. They just hung around talking to one another in subdued tones. Early the next morning another aircraft was heard passing overhead but we had no one on deck at that time to identify it. Later that day, however, a couple of chaps who had been at the latrines on deck shouted that a tug was approaching. From the ensuing yells and movements of the crew on the deck above us we surmised that lines were being passed across and sure enough, shortly afterwards, we felt the ship begin to move. It seemed that we were being towed at a faster speed than the little ship had managed under her own power and she creaked and groaned in protest. Nevertheless she held together and some twelve hours later we felt her slow down before being pushed gently up against something solid. The something solid turned out to be the quayside at the port of Takeo, a major Japanese naval base on the island of Formosa, which at that time was a Japanese colony. (Since independence the island has reverted to its former name of Taiwan and the port of Takeo is now Kaohsiung.) We arrived on New Year's Eve and the following day, 1 January 1944, was apparently a holiday for the Japs for they left us alone all day. We were allowed up on deck and could see and hear sounds of merriment (at least we took it to be merriment) coming from the surrounding ships.

Late the following morning two Japanese naval officers came aboard and shortly thereafter we were ordered to disembark. Getting out of the hold by climbing the one vertical ladder would have taken 300 fit men quite a while, but it took us a lot longer, which infuriated the guards. There were a number of civilians and sailors on the dockside watching the performance and I suppose the guards wanted to show off, but whatever the reason their shouting, kicking and liberal use of rifle butts reached new heights. When they eventually managed to get us all lined up on the dockside they had their usual difficulty in establishing that there were 300 of us, but when they were at last satisfied they handed us over to a new set of guards with a couple of sloppy salutes. The latter promptly counted us again, but doubtless in order to display their superior mathematical ability completed the headcount in about thirty seconds and marched us off along the quayside. We did not go very far before we were halted alongside a large merchantman which I judged to be between 10,000 and 12,000 tons. Her name, painted on her stern, was *Toyama Maru*, and when we were sent aboard via a gangplank leading to her upper deck I noticed that the brass centre-line marker plate stated that she had been built in Glasgow, Scotland in 1918. Again we were directed down below, only this time there were two holds so there was a lot more room. Furthermore, it was obvious that she had been used to transport troops in the past for there were "shelves" some 6 feet deep and raised 3 feet off the deck. These were lined with thin and not-too-clean bamboo matting. Some of the HK volunteers who were familiar with Japan said that the shelves and the matting-covered deck below were titamees, or sleeping platforms. Some troops would sleep on the deck and some on the "shelf" above. We did the same and compared with our previous ship this one gave us a lot more space. It was better in other ways too — there were, for example, reasonable toilet and cooking facilities — but most important, once we started moving, the engines emitted a smooth subdued rumble that sounded much healthier than the asthmatic wheezing of the little coastal steamer's engine.

The ship got under way shortly after we were embarked and a more relaxed set of guards permitted a few POWs at a time on deck. Again it was evening when my turn came and I could see that we were steaming north at a fair clip through a calm, lead-coloured sea. We were not in a convoy but were accompanied by a Japanese destroyer on a voyage that continued uneventfully for four days. Each time I was allowed on deck it was noticeably colder than the previous visit and the crew began wearing heavy coats. It seemed that Japan was our destination.

The ship eased into port late in the afternoon, we were ousted from the relatively warm hold and lined up on the quayside to shiver in what seemed to us, coming from sub-tropical Hong Kong, freezing temperatures. I had no idea where we were but there were among us men who had lived in Japan, and at least two who could speak the language and read written katakana text. They soon identified the place as the port of Moji on the southern island of Kyushu. After the usual ritual count we were crammed into trucks and taken across the narrow straights to Shimonoseld on the main island of Honshu. There we were dropped off at a railway station and lined up on the platform. It was bitterly cold. There was a chill wind blowing and as most of us were wearing threadbare uniforms that we had lived in since being captured, it seemed to go right through us. Why we did not all catch pneumonia I will never know. A clock on the opposite platform showed the time was 8.50p.m. when we arrived and we were still there when it registered 10.50. There were a number of Japanese civilians in the station and numerous inquisitive glances were made in our direction, but the guards discouraged

107

anyone getting too close. In fact, they forcibly drove them away shouting at them in much the same way as they did us, and I remember thinking that kind of behaviour was only to be expected under a military dictatorship.

At around eleven o'clock a passenger train drew into the platform where we stood and stopped in front of us. I did not think we would be boarding it for I was convinced in view of our recent experience of ocean cruising Japan-style that any overland transportation would be by cattle truck. However, I was wrong for after another hasty (I think the guards were cold too) count we were herded aboard into the welcome warmth of the carriages, where there was even space enough for many of us to sit down. The guards came through the carriages ensuring that all the blinds were drawn and threatening dire punishment if a blind was lifted or if anyone peeped out of a window. Considering the fact that it was pitch black outside and we could not see anything if the blinds had been lifted I thought their efforts were pretty stupid, unless it was a precaution against possible air raids which seemed unlikely for there had been no signs of a blackout on the station. Nevertheless the question of the blinds seemed to be a matter of great importance to the guards for they came through the carriages checking every ten minutes or so as the train rattled along through the night. They became even more agitated as light around the edges of the blinds indicated that dawn had arrived, but I never did ascertain what worried them so much about us looking out. Perhaps it was not so much us looking out as other people looking in and seeing a bunch of decrepit-looking occidentals travelling on their railways.

The train in which we were travelling was not an express. It stopped from time to time and could be heard and felt screeching around some tight bends. At a guess I would say it was averaging about 30 miles an hour, so when at last it stopped and we were ordered out around noon I reckoned we were some 350 to 400 miles from our starting point. In fact it was probably a little less for we were on the railway station in Nagoya where large indicator boards announced the station name in both English and Katakana.

We climbed stiffly out of the carriages, relieved to find it was not as cold as when we entered them. Again I noticed the guards kept civilians from getting anywhere near us which was probably just as well for we had been unable to wash for two weeks and a number of people suffering from dysentery had soiled their pants. We were all hungry and thirsty but the guards obviously had no intention of doing anything about that. They lined us up, did the ritual count and marched us off across the tracks to where a single railcar was parked. They literally rammed all 300 of us into it and then made room for themselves at the doorways. There was just not enough room to have both feet on the floor, but on the other hand we were so tightly packed there was no possibility of falling. Fortunately the journey under these cramped conditions lasted for only about fifteen minutes. The railcar stopped in the middle of what appeared to be open country and we squirted out on to the side of the track.

109

There were well-cultivated fields around from which came that characteristic, slightly acrid smell that accompanies the use of human manure. A narrow lane led away from the railway towards a hill a quarter of a mile distant and after yet another head count we were directed along it. We slowly trudged uphill to the accompaniment of shouts of "speedo speedo" from the guards and found that the lane wound round the side of the hill before climbing on up to a stockaded group of wooden buildings perched on the top. When we reached them the gates in the stockade were opened and we passed through into the camp where we were to spend the next seventeen months. It was officially known as "Osaka Number 8", although it was located about 5 miles from Nagoya, at a place called Narumi. For too many it was to be the last place they would know on earth.

For those who survived, however, it was not to be our final destination. In May 1945, Nagoya was heavily bombed by US long-range bombers. (We did not know then that they came from Saipan. The Japs called them "B ni jew que", Japanese for "B29".) Shortly afterwards we learned of Germany's surrender from stolen newspapers. This encouraged the optimists among us to declare that Japan would soon follow suit and it would not be long before we would be on our way home. Those surviving members of the Hong Kong University staff who knew the Japanese and could speak the language warned us not to get our hopes up. They said that the Japanese character, influenced by the Samurai tradition, was such that once committed to war they would fight until they either won or were destroyed — for them surrender was not an option. It seemed that they were right for suddenly the English contingent in the Narumi camp were given an order to be ready to move within twenty-four hours. So those of us who were left of the draft of 300 from Hong Kong said goodbye to our American friends, who wished us good luck, and prepared to move again. With very little warning we were marched down the hill and crammed (it was not so bad as on the first occasion we had climbed into it for so many had died in the meantime) into the little railcar that normally took us to work every morning. On this occasion, though, it did not stop at the kaisha (factory) where we provided the coolie labour, but proceeded on to Nagoya station and deposited us on a platform there. There were civilians on the same platform and again they were kept well away from us. A train came in and we were ordered to get aboard, only to find that all the blinds were down as before. The guards again insisted they stay that way but as we travelled in daylight and the zeal of the guards (this time for the most part young Koreans) was not quite up to the standard of those who accompanied us on our last rail journey, it was possible to sneak the odd look at the world outside. We were clearly going through mountainous country and the train went through a number of tunnels. What we could not determine was the direction we were taking, although there were numerous guesses as to our probable destination, with Tokyo as the favourite. If our knowledge of Japanese geography had been better we

111

would have known that there are no mountains between Nagoya and Tokyo, and if we were going through mountains we were probably going west. That is what we must have been doing for we eventually arrived and detrained at a place called Toyama, a city on Japan's west coast. We were marched to a camp about a quarter of a mile outside the town and that is where we were when the war ended nearly four months later. It was not until we were liberated that we were told that the quarter of a mile that separated us from the town had almost certainly saved our lives!

CHAPTER
EIGHT

On Public Hygiene

Before the war the Japanese had a reputation for being obsessed with both personal and public hygiene. They were known to soak themselves in communal hot baths, reputed to make a fetish of cleaning their teeth and always removed their shoes before entering a house. They were reported to maintain their streets in immaculate condition and to wear face masks at the slightest hint of infectious disease. But in Sham Shui Po they completely failed to live up to their reputation. Not even the simplest equipment was provided with which to keep the camp clean and although we did our best with what improvised brooms etc. that we were able to make we fought an unending battle against the flies. They settled on the tins, flower pots, upturned lamp shades and sundry other utensils that had been pressed into service as plates on which to receive our ration of boiled rice, and they were doubtless responsible for the rapid spread of dysentery throughout the camp.

When we arrived in Japan the attitude of the authorities differed markedly from those in Hong Kong. Gone was the indifference to conditions within the camp and in its place a strict set of rules aimed at keeping it spotlessly clean was introduced. I presumed that now we were on their turf and would be working in their factories the Japanese could not risk us infecting the locals. Brushes and brooms appeared; we were issued with white porcelain bowls and on one occasion toothbrushes, but regrettably neither toothpaste nor soap were forthcoming. Periodic inspections of the camp and its occupants were carried out by the Japanese Army Medical Corps, always on a yasumi day. It inevitably began with a long harangue about guarding one's health and the importance of keeping the camp clean. The speech was delivered by the senior Jap medical officer and translated by an interpreteur whose command of English was far from perfect and who from time to time made some humorous gaffs, although it was not funny when he made his greatest error and announced, "Today all men be castrated." It was a scary moment but fortunately what he meant was: "Today all men are to be vaccinated." Following the speech the huts were then fumigated with some evil-smelling spray and on a number of occasions we were lined up and inoculated, or on that one memorable day vaccinated. What we were inoculated against I do not know but some of the injections were very painful, especially the ones the Jap doctors insisted be given in the stomach.

During these inspections the Jap doctors always visited the medical hut and challenged the doctor's diagnosis of his patients. They came into the hut after I had been there four days with pneumonia and although

114

they did not contend that I was not suffering from that illness, they said I was sufficiently recovered to be discharged for camp duties. They also insisted that because my swollen legs showed all the signs of advanced beriberi I must be treated with their special remedy. This consisted of putting four small pyramids of incense-like paste on four specific spots on each leg and then setting them on fire. They smoldered for about ten minutes and then spluttered out. Unfortunately they did nothing to improve my condition but resulted in four sores on both legs, which took weeks to heal.

Another health fetish of the Japs was the rapid removal of the dead of which there were plenty, especially in the early days in Sham Shui Po when amoebic dysentery and diphtheria were rampant. Even though they would not permit medications to be brought into the camp they provided an endless supply of wooden coffins. Never a morning passed without a truck loaded with coffins, containing those who had died during the night, leaving for a burial ground.

In Japan the dead were cremated. When anybody died in the Narumi camp, and over a hundred did, the body was taken out of camp within hours to a burning ground about half a mile away. The body, wearing only a fandushi,[1] was placed on a two-wheel handcart which was pulled by two medical POWs and, if available, any sick POW confined to camp duties. Two guards accompanied the cart and on the first occasion that I was pressed into service they endeavoured to speed things up by shouting, "Spccdo, speedo" followed by the odd thump on the back with a rifle butt. At that

115

time I had some deep blisters filled with yellow puss in the balls of each foot and the journey to the burning ground was not only sad but painful. When we got there an old man stood before a pile of what looked like old thin planks of weather boarding taken from a demolished house. The body was placed directly on top of the pile, and a guard immediately lit a taper and applied it to the bottom of the pile. Flames soon shot up and engulfed the body, then to my horror one of its legs jerked and it seemed to raise an arm. The medics calmed me explaining that this kind of movement often happened as a result of tendons shrinking in the heat of the fire. Whilst the flames were still roaring and the body could still be seen, the guards made us pick up the cart again and return to camp. On the only other occasion I was available to assist in a cremation the guards were Korean. They made no attempt to speed things up and seemed to be pleased to be out of camp, so our progress to the burning ground was slow compared with the previous occasion. When we arrived the same old man was there with the same kind of woodpile as before. It stood, of course, on top of the ashes of many fires and as before the near-naked body was placed on top. This time the guards made no move to light a taper but, looking first at the body and then at us POWs, they kept saying something we could not understand. One of the medics said, "I think they want us to say a prayer or something for the deceased." This apparently was what was wanted for when we bowed our heads and said the Lord's Prayer (which was the only one we could think of at the time) the Koreans seemed pleased. One of them lit a taper and handed it to a medic, indicating that he was to light the fire. This he did and this time we were allowed to stay and watch for about half an hour as the flames began to consume the body.

Despite their insistence on cleanliness in the camp, the Japs did little to help us keep ourselves clean. There was a roofed-over ablution block in the camp with running cold water, but there was no soap. With sub-freezing temperatures in the winter one had to be a very hardy person to strip down and try to clean oneself in water that froze solid shortly after leaving the taps. Nor was one inclined to try to wash clothes in the freezing water because there was no way in which they could be dried. Not surprisingly, during the winter we confined our ablutions to a quick wipe over the face with a wet rag — what my mother would have called a lick and a promise. As a result, once the spring came most of us were infested with lice.

There was another practice of the Japs in Narumi that was anything but hygienic. The latrines and oblution troughs drained into a large open pit. Once a week villagers brought into camp a huge wooden tank suspended between two wheels. It was so constructed that the tank could be tipped over and emptied, and the whole contraption was pulled by a surly looking water buffalo. It was backed up to the latrine pit and the buffalo stood patiently still whilst its masters lifted the contents of the pit into the tank using king-sized bamboo ladles. Whilst marching to the railway halt we observed that in the corners of all the fields we passed

117

there were pits into which the excrement was deposited. There it stayed maturing until it was spread over the fields as fertilizer. When this happened the acrid smell permeated the atmosphere for days. It is a smell that is not easily forgotten and I knew exactly what it was and where I was when in 1960 I returned to Japan for the first time on business. The moment the doors of the aircraft were opened after landing in Tokyo it hit me, and even when ground staff came aboard and sprayed the cabin with a disinfectant (as was the Japanese practice at that time) it still lingered. It brought back all the memories and for the first few days of my stay I saw no Japanese civilians — my mind put them all back in uniform. It was a disturbing feeling but fortunately it passed, presumably when my subconscious accepted the fact that the war was over. In subsequent years I visited Japan on a number of occasions but I never again smelt that acrid smell nor suffered from the delusion that members of the Japanese armed forces surrounded me.

Note:
1. Fandushi — Japanese loincloth.

CHAPTER
NINE

On Camps and Coolies

Unlike Sham Shui Po, where we were not used as a source of free labour, Narumi and Toyama were very much working camps. This was made very clear to us when we first passed through the gate in the Narumi stockade to be met by a bunch of thugs presided over by the most evil and sinister-looking man I had ever seen. He was an army lieutenant, his support staff all army sergeants and we learned that they had all served and had been wounded in the war with China. Not fit for active service, they were given the prison camp posting, much to their disgust, and they took their frustration out on us. The Lieutenant's opening remark of his "welcoming" speech made through an interpreter was to the effect that he did not care whether we lived or died. There followed a bad-tempered tirade about the duties of prisoners and the dire results that would follow if we did not work "with all our might" in the service of the Japanese Empire and/or failed to bow to a Japanese soldier.

It became apparent early in our stay in Japan that the military personnel regarded themselves as some sort of elite. We, meanwhile, were hired out to a company in

Nagoya that manufactured railway locomotives. That company provided its own security guards, known to us as "stickmen", who accompanied us everywhere we went in the factory and on the journey to and from the camp. The sergeants on the camp administrative staff would have nothing to do with them and treated them with contempt. Even the young soldiers who comprised the armed guard within the camp and on the journey to and from the factory ignored them, and would speak to them only if it was absolutely necessary. We, of course, as far as the military was concerned, were an even lower form of life for we had committed the ultimate sin of surrender, something no Japanese soldier would ever consider doing. In the Camp Commandant's opinion we should not be alive, but as we were he intended to ensure that it would not be a pleasant life and ran the Narumi establishment as if it were a military punishment camp.

We were housed in two purpose-built huts, each about 30 yards long, with an ablution shed in between them. Inside each hut, tatamis at floor level and at 5 feet above ran down each side with a 6-foot-wide earth floor between them. The tatamis were 8 feet deep and each man was allocated a 2-foot by 6-foot space on them, leaving a 2-foot gangway along the front edges. It was here one sat, cross legged, for the last numbering session of the day, and the numbering, we were told on arrival, would be in Japanese. We were given just twenty-four hours in which to learn the Japanese numbers, after which anyone who failed to number in Japanese would be severely punished. In order to

120

comply we arranged to sit in the same position for every roll call, which meant that all we needed to do was remember just one number. A couple of practice runs ensured that everyone knew his number and when the first real count began it went very well until the numbering reached a group of Middlesex Regiment privates, all of whom were true cockneys from London's East End and were sitting on the upper tatami directly opposite to where I sat. When the numbering reached them the first man froze — his number had obviously gone out of his head — there was a moment of awkward silence, then with typical cockney quick-wittedness he rapidly improvised and shouted "hearts" whereupon the next man called "diamonds" and there followed "spades", "clubs" and "no trumps" in quick succession. It brought the house down for despite our perilous position the spontaneous burst of laughter was irrepressible. It drove the Japs mad and they lashed out at all and sundry with rifle butts and boots. They kept us sat there for another hour and a half by which time we had numbered correctly half a dozen times before they dismissed us with dire warnings on what would happen if we failed to number correctly in Japanese at the next roll call. The most worrying threat was that food would be withheld. In our state of near starvation that could have been disastrous and we made sure that the next day numbering in Japanese went smoothly. Howard Spring entitled his novel *Fame is the Spur* — in our case it was fear that motivated us, and for good reason. Men were already dying of starvation and from amoebic dysentery

121

that had followed us from Hong Kong. To be fair to the Japanese, though, it must be said that the food with which we were provided in Narumi was a slightly better quality than that received in Hong Kong, even though it was a bit less in quantity. It consisted of two small bowls of rice a day, which occasionally contained some unpolished rice and a few soya beans. Additionally, a small bread roll was provided that was meant to be eaten at the midday break at the kaisha (factory), and in the evening a small bowl of watery vegetable soup. This marginally improved diet did little to improve our health and I continued to suffer from beriberi, while the deep concave blisters in the soles of my feet would not go away, although by this time my feet seemed to have gone numb and I was not feeling much pain. The new diet may have retarded further deterioration.

After two days, in which we were taught not only to count in Japanese but also to bow in the correct Japanese manner, we were set to work. Used Japanese padded uniforms were issued which were very welcome for it was bitterly cold, and a few captured American Army boots were distributed. I managed to find a pair that more or less fitted and they proved a godsend to me for all I had was a pair of home-made wooden sandals. After the inevitable numbering performance, and clad in our new finery, we were marched off down the hill to the village railway halt, and there literally squeezed into a small railcar. This was done by the boots and rifle butts of the guards, to the accompaniment of their usual cacophony of grunts and squeals which served no useful purpose other than to confirm our conviction that we were in the hands of a bunch of sub-humans. Within the railcar there was insufficient room for everybody to have both feet on the floor, but on the other hand there was no danger of falling and one became closely aquainted with one's neighbours. The journey to Nagoya took about twenty minutes during which the whole mass of humanity was thrown first against one side of the railcar and then the other, as it rounded the sharper turns in the track. It was surprising that despite the liberal use of rifle butts to cram us into the car, and the way those situated next to the sides were crushed against them, on the whole of our stay at Narumi there were only a few cases of cracked ribs, and only two of broken arms.

When the car came to a halt in the railyards outside Nagoya station the doors were opened and we exploded onto the tracks, there to be herded by the stick men and the guards into the locomotive factory where we were to be used as unskilled and unpaid labourers. We were divided into five groups and allocated to various parts of the establishment such as the boiler shop, the machine shop, the fitting shop, the forge and in my case Group 1, known as the "odds and sods" group, which did any and every job that came up in the yards outside the various shops. In the course of our sojourn working for the locomotive company, Number 1 group performed a myriad of different jobs, none of which required any degree of skill or intelligence. However, there were a couple of tasks that are worth recalling. One was helping the factory charcoal maker. He was an interesting character who differed markedly from the

123

run-of-the-mill factory honchos (foremen). He must have been in his late twenties or early thirties, had very little sight in one eye, which presumably kept him out of military service, and moved lethargically. There was about him a sickly paleness and it is possible that he was suffering from some debilitating illness such as tuberculosis. We noticed that he was always alone, and never saw another Japanese come up and speak to him, except for the stickmen when they delivered us, and even they shot off the moment they had handed us over. We all felt a little sorry for him, particularly so because compared with the bombastic attitude of many of the honchos he was very mild mannered and never pushed us. The job involved cutting up wood, which for the most part consisted of the outer trimmings, including the bark, from tree trunks that were in the process of being turned into timber in a nearby lumber company, and stacking it under his expert direction. He would often spend the whole afternoon sitting back on a pile of wood and leave us to our own devices. The finished pile was a partial sphere some 30 feet in diameter and 6 feet high at the centre. We covered it with sod, old tarpaulins or anything else the honcho could find. He would then demonstrate how to light it and when this was accomplished to his satisfaction we would be dismissed to work elsewhere for a week or so, before returning to dismantle the pile and start the process all over again. One became very dirty dismantling and stacking a pile of charcoal and when we were finished our friendly honcho permitted us to use an adjacent water standpipe to clean ourselves up

124

as best we could. Close by was a bench on which several honchos would sometimes sit to eat their lunch during the midday break; occasionally one or two of them would forget the rules and leave the newspaper they had been reading or in which they had wrapped their "bento boxes". Because of our honcho's poor vision and his habit of dozing off in the afternoon, it was easy to pick up those papers without being noticed and stuff them into our trousers on the inside of the thigh. In that position they avoided detection when we were searched on return to camp and no one was ever caught committing the heinous crime of smuggling in newspapers. Once in the camp two of our number could translate the Japanese text and the news they gleaned was rapidly spread by word of mouth after the papers had been destroyed.[1] Unfortunately this rich source of newspapers dried up late in 1944 just as the weather was turning cold, for we were no longer called upon to help the charcoal maker. Apparently he had died and there was no one to replace him. By that time we had become quite conversant with the process, but the Japs would not trust us to do the job on our own which was perhaps a wise decision on their part for, given the opportunity, we were not above indulging in a little of what we liked to think of as sabotage which, although very minor, gave our moral a lift.

Such an opportunity arose when on one occasion ten of us were taken by two stickmen to a section of the factory we had not previously visited. There we were put to work unloading from a barge thirty small phosphor-bronze, three-bladed propellers that had

125

been made in Germany. They were some 9 inches in diameter and each was encased in a wooden frame. Our job, once we had taken them out of the barge, was to break them out of their cases and store them on shelves in a nearby warehouse. In the course of doing this we noticed that each propeller had three grub screws with which to secure it to the propeller shaft and that these screws were also made of phosphor bronze, a metal which it was felt certain Japan did not possess at that time. Furthermore, we were convinced that the propellers were destined for Japanese human torpedo boats (small, high-speed motorboats fitted with a large explosive charge in the bow that were designed to be driven right into the target). We were not being closely watched and it occurred to us that if we could remove all the grub screws without being caught no one would be any the wiser, for whoever came to collect the propellers would assume that the grub screws had not been provided and the chances were that mild steel screws would be substituted. As these could deteriorate in salt water they would hopefully fail at a critical moment; such was our thinking at the time. If the plan was to succeed obviously all the screws had to be removed, but with the bored stickmen sitting outside in the sunshine and no one watching what we did inside the warehouse, this did not appear to be too difficult. We knew that the screws were loose and could be turned by putting a thumbnail in the slot, so we decided to have a go and proceeded to remove them. They came out easily and we had dealt with twenty-eight propellers when the stickmen got up and walked into the warehouse. There was a tense couple of minutes but as the last two uncrated propellers were brought into the warehouse, the stickmen exhorted us to "speedo speedo", indicated we were to move elsewhere and walked outside again. With the panic over the screws were surreptitiously dropped into the murky waters near the barge and we went on our way. Our little effort obviously had no major effect on the course of the war but nevertheless we held our heads a little higher when we returned to camp that night.

Such little boosts to moral, even though they might be the result of wishful thinking, did help sustain us. We were worked for twenty-eight continuous days when we first started at Narumi, and then were given one yasami day (holiday) in which to clean up the camp and ourselves. After that, one yasami day every two weeks was permitted and on such occasions we did what we could to clean our clothes and rid ourselves of the lice which had become a problem. The continuous work program coupled with the inadequate food supply took its toll. The body seemed to have just enough energy to get through the day's routine, but any abnormal demand on it spelt trouble. Thus chaps who developed dysentery, influenza or any other form of illness, or were beaten up by the guards (a not uncommon experience), did not seem to have the strength to fight the illness or their injuries, and many a man died from ailments which in normal health they would have shrugged off. The Japanese reaction involved a couple of visits by their military doctors, but all they did was force us to have painful injections in the stomach and to burn small pieces of what looked like incense on various points of one's leg. None of these miracle cures did much for our health and people continued to die at an alarming rate, so much so that by the end of 1944 we had lost nearly 20 per cent of those who had arrived in Japan nearly a year earlier. Presumably to make up for these losses, early in the New Year, after two more huts were constructed, we were joined by 300 American POWs. The newcomers were from the Philippines and some of them were survivors of the infamous Bataan death march. They updated us as to what had happened in the Philippines and told us that General MacArthur had slipped away at the last moment, but they had little news since their capture. So we were able to inform them about what we had gleaned from the Japanese newspapers. This was not altogether bad news for although the Japanese were still reporting (quite inaccurately) huge victories in New Guinea and Australia, the reports about what was happening in North Africa and Russia were, as I have subsequently discovered, fairly accurate, indicating that the tide was beginning to turn.

The arrival of the American POWs necessitated some changes in the camp routine. In order to make better use of the available inadequate facilities their timetable was set at one hour after ours; thus whilst we were up at six and in the railcar by seven, they were up at seven and in the railcar by eight. Conversely, whilst we arrived back in camp at six they came in an hour later. They took over the work previously done by Group 1 leaving us members of that group to be reallocated. I found myself together with a member of the Hong Kong Volunteer Defence Force, who in a previous life had been the Chief Engineer of the Hong Kong Light and Power Company, handed over to the tender mercies of one of what hitherto we had referred to as the "barrow boys". These were the coolies who pushed or pulled large, heavy, two-wheeled, steel barrows around the factory moving supplies and materials from one shop to another. I suspect that with the arrival of the Americans the factory management found itself with a surfeit of unskilled labour, otherwise it would not have allocated two of us to a barrow without releasing the original operator for other work. On the other hand it is problematical whether our newly acquired honcho was capable of other work. He was a frightening figure when we first beheld him and as he led us away with the barrow shouting and indicating that we were to follow, I was filled with apprehension. He was a dark and swarthy character only about 5 feet 2 inches high, his shoulders were enormously broad and his strong muscular arms were so long that when he stood upright his wrists fell level with his knees. He babbled away all the time in a language that we could not understand and I suspect nor could the Japanese who, except for the young ones, who occasionally shouted at him, avoided him whenever they could. He was permanently dirty, his black tunic and trousers were in rags and he had the very disconcerting habit of suddenly, without any warning, throwing up his head and howling like a dog. Inevitably we called him the "missing link".

With him leading us and making noises which we at first took to be demands to move faster, we filled the barrow with lime, coal, iron ore or scrap metal, pulled it up the circular ramp to the top of the blast furnaces and dumped it for the Japanese furnace men to load in due course. We then rolled back downhill to the foundry to pick up still warm castings and take them to the machine shops. We took their products to the finishing and assembly shop where the locomotives were built, and then started the circuit all over again. There were times when the two of us had insufficient strength to pull the heavily laden barrow over some of the bumps and holes in the track, or to load the heavier castings. When this happened the "link's" babbling would move into high pitch, he would jump up and down and then push us aside in order to demonstrate how easy it was for a real man to accomplish the task. It was all rather frightening at first but unlike other honchos he never attempted to strike us or call the stickmen and we soon learned to encourage these displays of physical superiority. So much so that by the time we were moved from Narumi in May 1945 a labour-sharing modus operandi had been developed whereby he pulled the barrow over the rough ground and up the ramp whilst we pulled on the level sections of the circuit. Similarly, he loaded and unloaded the heavy castings whilst we dealt with the machined parts. I am fairly certain he knew what we were doing but having seen the way he was treated by the stickmen and his fellow workers, especially the young men who used to taunt him, I suspect he felt more rapport with us than with them. Although we were guilty of exploiting his limited mental capacity we were his constant companions, something he had not had before, we talked to him as best we could and treated him like a normal human being. He revealed his feelings the last day we were at the Nagoya factory when he came up to us as we were leaving and said something which we presumed was "goodbye", so we said "goodbye", whereupon he grabbed us each by the hand and gently squeezed. Then he turned away and ran off, but before he turned we saw tears running down his face — I think he knew he was alone again and I could not help feeling sorry for him.

American aircraft were seen over Nagoya during the early months of 1945 and there was some bombing. Following one raid we were confined to camp for a day, presumably so that we would not see the extent of the damage, or because power supplies had been interrupted. When we returned to work the factory did not appear to have been hit but it was clear that the station and adjacent railway lines had been, and probably on more than one occasion. In the factory evidence of lack of materials was showing up, there was little for us to do, the blast furnaces were idle and the Japanese were beginning to show a degree of war weariness. They no longer showed that zealous enthusiasm for work that they had displayed when we first arrived. Even the banzai parties they gave when one of their number went off to join the armed forces lacked lustre, possibly because by now the only ones left to be called up were youngsters in their early teens.

131

Then, early in May 1945, there were some very heavy air raids on Nagoya and we were confined to camp for three days in a row. When we returned to work the factory was still undamaged as far as we could see but the workers were obviously worried. A few days later on return to camp we were told that some time after the next yasami day we would be moved. Although not surprising the announcement was nevertheless disappointing for the news we had optimistically hoped for was an announcement of an armistice. Only the week before the Japanese papers had published the news of Germany's surrender.

Leaving our American friends behind in Narumi, the 180 or so of us that were left were moved at the end of May 1945 to Toyama on Japan's west coast. Here the Nagoya locomotive company had a subsidiary company that manufactured steamrollers to an English design laid out on blueprints dated 1912. We were housed in what had previously been some kind of monastery or religious school around which a wooden stockade had been hastily erected. We had a little more room than in Narumi and instead of the daily commute by railcar in Toyama, all we had to do was march a quarter of a mile down a narrow track between two paddy fields to reach the factory. As a result we did not leave the camp until 7.45 a.m. and were back not later than 5.30, which gave us a little more time to ourselves. The work in the factory was less arduous than in Nagoya. We were given the jobs which I imagine would have been done by the apprentice boys if they had any left, but this factory had no young men — it was populated by the elderly. I was made to work on a planing machine and my job was to take the rough edges off an ingot. I had to plane it down to a line marked on it and then the machinist would take over. He must have been well into his sixties but he still managed to operate four machines. He somehow explained what he wanted and every time I cut below the prescribed mark, which I frequently did, he would hit me on the head with the edge of a steel ruler for ruining the piece. I got back at him when sent to the grinding wheel to sharpen a tool. I surreptitiously scooped up a handful of emery dust and poured it into the machine's lubricating system. Compared with the operations in the Nagoya factory when we first arrived, the pace in Toyama was leisurely. Everybody seemed tired and not one steamroller was completed during the whole four months we were there. We were quite pleased with the new conditions in which we found ourselves; the only fly in the ointment being the Camp Commandant who had come with us from Narumi. Known to all simply as "the Bastard", his brooding, malevolent presence still hung over us. We noted with some concern his interest in the construction, by the local civilian population, of pillboxes made of bamboo and clay at every intersection we could see on our way to work. However, he was not accompanied by his sadistic administrative staff and the NCOs who ran the Toyama camp were a much more reasonable bunch. So, telling ourselves "it will not be long now", we settled down to await the day of liberation and prayed that it would come soon. More serious effects of malnutrition than we had experienced hitherto were beginning to raise their ugly head. Some people, myself included, were beginning to lose their sight. Whatever one looked at became a circle of white light and only objects on the periphery of the field of vision were visible. It seemed to us therefore that unless we were rescued soon our chances of survival were diminishing daily. Fortunately, we were unaware that before the day of release arrived we were to be visited by an armada of B29s on a massive fire-bombing raid, and that in the camp office there were written orders from Tokyo Headquarters that all prisoners of war were to be killed immediately in the event of an invasion of the Japanese home islands![2]

Notes:

1. Newspapers. Whilst newspapers were smuggled in without detection, the greatest danger was being caught with them inside camp during one of the surprise searches the Japs were fond of making. Consequently as soon as a paper was inside the huts it was divided between the two translators who took their pieces with them into the latrines. There they translated the papers and memorized their content before tearing them up and dropping the pieces into the evil-smelling mess below. Because of our rice diet everybody in the camp had to get up and urinate at least twice each night, so by the time the farmers came on their weekly visits to collect the human manure, the pieces of paper were degraded and became part of the ghastly, acrid-smelling slime that they stored in pits at the corners of their fields to

allow it to "mature".

On one occasion, however, a search of the huts was started almost as soon as we had returned from the factory and before we had completed the usual bowing routine. This had never happened before — they usually left us alone for an hour after returning from the kaisha so that both their food and ours could be distributed. Perhaps the guards suspected that we had smuggled something in without being detected or maybe they were just being their usual bloody-minded selves. Whatever it was it caused a bit of a panic. Disaster was averted, however, by the quick thinking of the two chaps who had newspapers stuffed inside their trousers — they tore them up and eat them!

2. Although throughout Japan and elsewhere at the time of the surrender the Japs destroyed these and other incriminating documents, an Allied search team on Formosa discovered an only slightly singed copy of the "execute" order. Also found were instructions to "Personnel who mistreated prisoners of war and internees or are held in extremely bad sentiment by them are permitted to take care of it by immediately transferring or by fleeing without trace." A vivid description as to how these documents were found is contained in Jack Edwards' graphic and gripping account of his experiences as a POW in Formosa entitled *Banzai You Bastards*, published by Corporate Communications, Hong Kong.

CHAPTER
TEN

On News and Newspapers

All types of prisoners suffer from the loss of liberty and to an extent are cut off from the outside world, but few are so completely cut off as are prisoners of war. They are removed from the scene of violent action and left wondering what might be happening on other fronts and over the progress of the war in general. When we were first taken prisoners the Jap guards were pleased to keep us informed. They boasted about Pearl Harbor and how they were overrunning the Philippines, Malaya and the Dutch East Indies. They claimed that they were already invading Australia and were on their way through Burma to India where they expected to meet up with their German allies who were already in Alexandria. When this happened it would not be long before they would conquer America and England and they were eagerly looking forward to raping all the girls in London and New York. To prove their point they even allowed into camp English language newspapers containing reports to the effect that Rommel had taken Alexandria and crossed the Nile en route for India, Darwin had been heavily bombed and a Japanese army had landed in northern Australia. Even when taken with a grain of salt this news was to say the least disconcerting and in what I suppose was an act of self-preservation a whole crop of counter rumours began to circulate. They were much more optimistic, the favourite being that a massive Chinese army was moving south to relieve Hong Kong; it was even rumoured that the army was lead by Chang Kai Shek himself, riding a white horse!

Needless to say the internal rumours were even less accurate than the Japs' stories but as we were living in what might be termed a news vacuum, inevitably rumour or "buzzes", as we called them, would emerge to fill the empty space. They became much more frequent after the first guards, who had been drawn from the invading front-line troops, were replaced in the spring of 1942 by recent recruits. These young soldiers had obviously been ordered not to talk to us and the English language paper was no longer allowed into camp. Rumour then held sway until the summer when NCOs started coming round the huts occasionally in the evening with what was termed a "news bulletin". They never said where it came from, only that we must not discuss it anywhere near a Jap, and if ever questioned never disclose that we had the information. With the advent of this, what we thought to be authentic news, the rumour mill subsided but it started up again some months later when the "news bulletins" ceased. As I was in the diphtheria hut at the time it was not until much later that I learned what happened. Apparently our news bulletins were put together by a group who had managed to build a radio and rigged an aerial. This home-made set was apparently capable of picking up Allied broadcasts, particularly at night. In order to minimize the risk of discovery during the fairly frequent surprise searches the Japs were in a habit of conducting, the radio equipment was divided, I believe, into five parts, each hidden separately by the members of the group. It was only brought together and operated on nights when it was considered safe to do so. All went well until during a search one part was found in the possession of the leader of the group, a young Lieutenant of the Royal Scots. The Japs took him away and questioned him about where the rest of the equipment was and who else was involved. He declined to oblige them and despite the most hideous torture they never broke him. He died without betraying his comrades, ten days after being caught with the incriminating piece of equipment. The Japs carried out numerous other searches throughout the camp and for days on end had all the prisoners standing on the parade ground whilst the searches were being made. However they never found the other parts of the radio or the people who had hidden them. After the war, the Lieutenant, whose courage was an inspiration to us all for he had literally laid down his life for his friends, was posthumously awarded the George Cross.

With the demise of the news bulletins we had no source of information on what was happening in the outside world. Nevertheless those bulletins had given us hope for they showed that the situation was not as bad as the Japs would have us believe. They had, for example, lost a major naval battle in the Coral Sea and although they might have made an ineffective air raid on Darwin, they had not landed in Australia. In fact, according to our bulletins they were bogged down in New Guinea. They were still fighting in New Guinea when we managed to find a new source of information: the newspapers we picked up in the Nagoya factory. Remembering how the Japs had boasted when we were first taken prisoner we tended to be sceptical about Japanese newspaper reports. Looking back after the war, though, it seemed that their reporting on the war in Europe, Africa and Russia was fairly accurate, if a little out of date. Their reporting on their own war in the East, however, was anything but accurate — they were still invading Australia in July 1945 and winning major naval battles in the Pacific when an American fleet was already bombarding the coastline of the Japanese home islands.

Because we had cause to discount the news of the war in the East, we were inclined to do the opposite with newspaper reports of fighting in Europe and Russia. Thus when we learned that the Russians had won a major battle at Stalingrad, we envisaged that they were already at the gates of Berlin. To calm our excitement some of the Hong Kong Volunteers, who in civil life comprised the academic staff of Hong Kong University, pointed out the vast distance between the two cities. It was not until some unknown and unpronounceable place names began to appear, which the geography professor recognized as towns in Poland, that they accepted that the fall of Berlin was imminent. By that time, however, the Japanese had already reported the Normandy landings and the fall of Paris — the prevailing view among us POWs was that the war would be over before winter set in and that we would be home for Christmas. Of course it was not and when the festive season arrived we were still in the prison camp privately wondering whether we could survive another year. Some did not.

Whilst we were at Narumi we were permitted to send two postcards to relatives and on two occasions we received short notes from home. Because of the severe censorship neither we nor those who wrote to us could say much, but nevertheless the communications we did receive contained some of the most important news of all. They confirmed that our families in war-torn Britain were alive and had not been killed in a German air raid (at that time we were unaware of the V1 and VII rockets). On the first occasion that mail was received in Narumi I had two letters, and on the second three. Each time the latest letter was over eighteen months old; all five were from my mother telling me of my siblings' progress at school and that everything was all right at home. The chap who slept next to me on the tatami was a petty officer motor mechanic who had been sent to Hong Kong to help maintain the engines of the MTBs. He was some twelve years older than me and before joining the Navy had owned and operated a garage in Manchester. He was a likable character, endowed with a cheerful disposition and a large dose of common sense. When the second lot of mail arrived he was overjoyed to receive seven letters: six from his wife and one from his sister. Some were over two years old

140

and even the latest, the one from his sister, had been posted eighteen months previously. He sorted them into chronological order and rushed to read them before lights out. I remember that he laughed a couple of times and said his children, of which he had three, must be growing like weeds for the eldest girl was already as tall as her mother. Then he picked up his sister's letter; as he began to read he let out a little groan and lay back on the tatami looking very pale. He pushed the letter into my hand without a word, but I had only to read the very first sentence to feel his pain. In it his sister said she was sorry to have to inform him that his wife and two younger children had been killed in an air raid, but the eldest girl was all right because she had been staying with her grandmother in the country the weekend the raid took place. There was nothing I or anybody else could do to comfort him. I heard him sobbing in the night and when a guard clanging a triangle sounded reveille, I had to shake him to wake him up. To my dismay he did not wake for he was dead and his body already cold. The night before he was as fit as anybody in thc camp could be, which is perhaps not saying much, but nevertheless the spirit of life was there whilst it had a vision to which it could cling. With that vision removed the spirit died and with it the will to live. I have often wondered since whether he would still be alive if his sister had not written that fateful letter. As the old adage says: there are times when ignorance is bliss and 'tis folly to be wise.

CHAPTER
ELEVEN

On Commerce and Courage

I suppose that the hereditary make-up of some men includes a need to trade, for we had not been in Sham Shui Po for more than a couple of weeks when people started exchanging things, and one bright lad, who hailed from a line of famous city merchant bankers and was the son of a noble lord, started a business in empty bottles. Others followed his lead and soon there were markets in empty bottles and tins, watches, eating utensils and pieces of clothing. The common currency that oiled the wheels of this underground economy was cigarettes, and this immediately distinguished the rich from the poor. The former were those who either had the foresight to drag large quantities of cigarettes into camp with them or were members of the Hong Kong Volunteers whose relatives, friends or former servants were permitted to bring them parcels of food and cigarettes; the latter were the rest of us. This happy state of affairs lasted for the first three months of our captivity, during which the camp guards were drawn from the original invaders. When these were withdrawn and replaced by younger and less experienced troops, parcels were banned and the cigarette economy was seriously endangered. However some intrepid souls found a new source of supply and they began exchanging wristwatches for cigarettes with some of the guards. The latter were for the most part young conscripts, some of whom were only too delighted to swap cigarettes surreptitiously for expensive-looking watches. (It would have been impossible to do this with the original guards for if they saw a watch on a prisoner's wrist they were known to snatch it off.)

With a reduced source of supply the available "currency" became more valuable and anyone who still possessed cigarettes was rich indeed. By then, however, most of us had overcome our longing for a cigarette and the only members of the naval group who had any were the old hands from the boom defence vessel. They were an enterprising lot and had set up a laundry service. Of course there was no soap available but by collecting the wood ash from the camp cookhouse and soaking it in water, which they then siphoned off, they produced a caustic soda solution which was a good cleaning agent, even if tough on the hands. Their operation was very well organized. Two of them went round the "rich" parts of camp seeking business, collecting dirty laundry and delivering newly laundered items. These two were responsible for collecting payment and for marking garments to ensure they went back to their rightful owners. Two others collected and processed the wood ash, or lye as they called it, and the rest did the laundering. They achieved quite a reputation for the quality of their work and their reliability. Also, and very much to their credit, they never smoked a cigarette in the hut where we all lived, and from time to time they gave a cigarette or two to naval types in the "hospital huts".

Their business was still going strong when I left Hong Kong, but by that time the "currency" had received two inputs. Firstly, in June or July 1942, by which time most people had overcome any hankering after a cigarette, the Japs suddenly allowed enough cigarettes into camp to permit a packet of ten to be issued to each man — just sufficient to awake the longing all over again as most of us smoked them since they relieved the pangs of hunger. The next input came the following year when to our great delight we each received an American Red Cross parcel. The existence of these parcels had been rumoured for some time, for it was known that a ship bearing a large Red Cross on her side had been seen in the harbour several months before. It was thought that she came from or was going to Lourenco Marques, the Mozambique port on the south-east coast of Africa. It was there, it was believed, that an exchange of diplomatic personnel and very sick civilians had or was to take place. In any event, although I am not certain exactly how the parcels reached Hong Kong, I am quite sure no parcel has ever been more welcome. They contained little tins of meat, butter and fruit, enriched chocolate bars, instant coffee, a tube of brushless shaving cream (which I ate on my rice) and two packs of Chesterfield cigarettes. The latter item soon revived the flagging underground economy and in a matter of hours a "market price" in cigarettes had been established for every item the Red Cross had sent us. Even so, despite the fact that they could easily have traded their ration of cigarettes for food, there were two non-smokers among the naval contingent who chose not to do so. Instead, they distributed their cigarettes between their close friends and the very sick in the "hospital huts." Considering we were all starving at the time one can but admire such men.

The move to Japan put an end to this "commercialism" for we took with us only what we stood up in and nobody had anything with which to trade. Furthermore, the physical demands placed upon us, coupled with the inadequacy of our rations both in quantity and quality, left us with very little energy to spare for frivolous matters. We had just sufficient energy to get through the day, and any demand over and above the normal routine left us exhausted. Such demands came though, and one of the most annoying was when we were kept on parade after returning from work. Normally we would be marched into camp and lined up on the parade ground whilst we were counted and searched. Then we would be turned to face in the direction of Tokyo and made to bow three times to the Emperor, whilst we were supposed to be saying "kairai, kairai, kairai", although in fact we usually managed to say something quite different and unprintable. When we had satisfactorily performed this salute to the Sun God we would be dismissed until final roll call and lights out. On occasion, however, when the guards had found something during a search, were not satisfied with our numbering or our bows to the Emperor, or were just in a bad mood, they would keep us standing to attention for half an hour or so until our legs were aching and one or two of our number had collapsed; they would then make us repeat the bowing process over and over again. By the time we were eventually dismissed it could be anything up to two hours after marching in and everybody would be in poor shape. The only way we could relieve our frustration was by muttering under our breath "Churchill, Roosevelt, Stalin" every time we bowed. On one occasion we muttered a little too loudly and were heard by one of the sadistic camp administrative staff who we had nicknamed "Fishface". He immediately had the guards call us to attention and through the Jap interpreter demanded to know, "Who said that?" There was an ominous silence and our hearts fell, for it seemed that we were in for a long session on the parade ground. Then suddenly, to everyone's surprise, a voice boldly said, "I did." The voice was that of a Eurasian member of the Hong Kong Defence Force, not a man who I would have expected to be associated with an act of self-sacrifice. He had hitherto been a quarrelsome character with a permanent chip on his shoulder and I had not much cared for him but that evening he displayed more courage than the rest us, for admission of guilt meant a nasty beating up. He was taken into the guardhouse and we were dismissed to ponder his fate. Much to our amazement, however, he was released within ten minutes after just a few slaps across the face which was the kind of punishment the Japs meted out to their own troops for a minor offence. Apparently when he was taken into the guardhouse Fishface was called away so

146

the guard corporal administered a couple of quick slaps and sent our man on his way. He was lucky — had Fishface himself conducted the beating it is probable that our Eurasian friend would have had to be carried back to our huts. All the same, I regarded him in a different light from then on for what he had done was the action of a very brave man and he had spared the rest of us two hours misery on the parade ground.

Because there was such little food available every grain of rice counted and to ensure fair distribution a code of conduct evolved. We had each been provided with a porcelain bowl and lid, and at morning and evening meal times these were put on the narrow trestle tables that ran down the centre of the huts. Two members of each mess would then go to the cookhouse where tubs of rice for each mess were displayed and if it was agreed by all that each tub contained the same amount of rice the "cooks of the mess" would pick up their tubs and return to the huts with them. There it was the duty of the "cooks" to fill each bowl with exactly the same amount and when that was done to the satisfaction of all the members we each took our own bowl. The rice was cooked over wood fires in two large woks, but inevitably some was burnt on the woks and had to be scraped off. This burnt rice was also subject to the conduct code and was distributed to each mess in turn. As there were eight messes it meant that this little extra arrived every eighth day and the receiving mess distributed it equitably among its members after the evening meal. It gave one something to look forward to and this, together with the daily

147

bread roll, was responsible for the revival of commercial activity. This time, although a "not-for-profit" operation, it was something akin to a futures market. What happened was that chaps would offer up their roll or burnt rice for repayment at a later date. In this manner some would, for example, give up their roll on two not necessarily consecutive days, and by making deals with two separate individuals arrange to receive two rolls back all on one day, thus ensuring that for once they had enough to eat. I used the system to ensure that I had two rolls on the occasion of my twenty-fourth birthday. The "market" became very active when the rolls were distributed early in the morning and again when the burnt rice was distributed in the evening. On one such occasion I recall seeing a very senior bank official and the managing director of a major shipping line arranging a burnt rice deal with all the seriousness they might have applied to negotiating a loan to build a new ocean liner. I felt what an incongruous situation it was, but then we lived in an incongruous world. For example, on yasami days, at the Japs' insistence, hot water was put in a container not much larger than an oil drum and the whole camp was expected to take a bath in it. On one infamous yasami day some inebriated guards came into camp and insisted that we have a concert. When they realized our reluctance to perform the situation became ugly and they started lashing out with rifle butts and one or two snapped on their bayonets. At that point a RAF Sergeant named Bunny Austin stepped forward and in a somewhat quivering voice started singing "Begin the Beguine";

the rest of us immediately did our best to follow him. His action saved the day for having got us going the guards seemed satisfied and slunk off. In all the years that have passed since that "concert" I have never heard that song played without thinking of Bunny Austin and the courage he displayed on that day long ago in Narumi. The scene is still as fresh in my mind as if it happened yesterday.

CHAPTER
TWELVE

On Earthquakes and Attitudes

We were fortunate in Narumi to have among us professors from Hong Kong University who were knowledgeable in Japanese culture and history. From them we learned that the Japanese were a very proud race who traditionally considered all other peoples to be inferior. So much so that a Japanese with the most menial occupation would be thankful that he was Japanese when he saw a foreigner pass by, even if that foreigner was obviously a man of great wealth and importance. They tended to lead somewhat ascetic, Spartan lives aimed at building the strength of character necessary to shoulder the many obligations that their hierarchical society placed upon them. The civilians we came across in both the Nagoya and Toyama factories in which we worked showed some of these characteristics. I had thought they were being arrogant, but apparently it was just their nature to think that as Japanese they must be superior.

"If they think about us at all," one professor said, "they probably consider that our very presence confirms their ascendancy because under their code to be taken prisoner is the greatest disgrace and death is much to be preferred."

The same professor alleged that much of Japanese culture flowed directly from the strict feudal system that had prevailed until the end of the last century. In recent years, however, it had been reinforced by the Shinto religion,[1] which the militarists had strongly supported and had made the official state religion when they obtained political control in the early 1930s. As a technique for influencing people's thinking, Shintoism, with its bushido militaristic philosophy, was probably more effective than any of Dr Goebbels's propaganda efforts in support of the Nazi Party in Germany. It emphasized the need for strict obedience to authority and for self-sacrifice, and its influence could be seen in the factory shops. There was obviously a rigid line of authority with the lower rank bowing lower to a superior than the latter's return bow, but more importantly the influence was shown in the zeal with which the workers applied themselves to their tasks. By the end of 1944 they must have known that the war was not going well for them, but there was no slackening of effort and no lack of self-confidence, at least until the afternoon of 8 December when we were still employed in the Nagoya factory.

The day had begun normally enough, with the usual march to the village rail halt, the trip in the railcar (by now not quite so crowded as death had trimmed our numbers), the morning's three rounds of the circuit with the barrow followed by the lunch break. Then, when we had just reached the assembly shop on the first of the afternoon circuits, an earthquake struck.

151

There was a loud roar as if an express train was thundering towards us; suddenly all that had been solid and static for the whole of one's life seemed to turn into a liquid and we were tossed from side to side as if we were standing in a rowing boat on a choppy sea. The tall brick chimneys at the far end of the factory buckled in the middle and momentarily looked like huge letters "S" before crumbling to the ground. Smoke from the small foundry shop flowed horizontally out of the windows instead of vertically out of the chimneys — I was not only scared stiff but felt seasick as well. I was not alone — the Japs came screaming out of the shops, guards and stickmen hurtled past us and although I never saw where the "Link" went, most people seemed to head for an open area where railway lines were stored, so we stumbled after them. As we did a second quake struck and telephone lines strung between the few poles that remained standing, albeit at a drunken angle, swung rapidly from side to side as though they were being shaken. We reached the open area where the Japs had gone but we could just as easily have walked out of the main gate. At that moment nobody was interested in us as they were too concerned with saving their own skins. The guards, who on that day happened to be a bunch of Koreans serving in the Jap Army, were clearly as scared as we were. When a series of after shocks began about twenty minutes after the two main quakes, they disappeared together with some Japanese civilian workers in search of a safer haven. My barrow partner and I stayed put for the majority of the workforce had not moved and we thought they probably knew that our present location was as safe as any. They were obviously very apprehensive though, and one or two did the unheard of and came over and spoke to us. We could not understand what they said but their sign language indicated that we had experienced an earthquake and their high-pitched laughter showed how nervous they were. I could sympathize with that for I found the earthquake far more frightening than the shelling we experienced in Hong Kong. The two main quakes probably lasted only for a few seconds but it felt like minutes for all one's lifelong reference points disappeared and the sense of balance was lost. There was nowhere to go to hide from it or to get out of its way and one became disorientated. To use a colloquial but appropriate expression for a moment: we did not know which way was up.

Everybody stayed in the open area for about an hour after the quake struck. Then when there had been no minor after shocks for about twenty minutes people began to move to assess the damage. We drifted after them and saw that except for the power station, where the chimneys had collapsed, most buildings seemed to have come through unscathed. There were fires burning in a couple of places and with all power off a strange quiet hung over the whole factory. We joined a crowd peering into the gloom of the assembly shop. A fine dust covered everything and the two huge locomotives that had been standing on trestles and were about to be "married" to their sets of wheels had fallen to the floor where they lay on their sides looking like a pair of beached whales.

Two rather shame-faced stickmen found us there and herded us along to the assembly area near the main gate. Here we found most of our people and some decidedly worried guards. They kept counting us until they were satisfied that we were all there and that none had escaped. Then they wandered around talking rapidly to each other, obviously at a loss as to what to do next. There was no power and therefore no railcar, the factory was temporarily out of action so what were they to do with us? The question was answered by the timely arrival of one of the camp administrative staff, the one who spoke a little English. He arrived on a bicycle and promptly tore a strip off the guards, slapping the Corporal across the face half a dozen times. He then turned his attention to the stickmen and harangued them for a few minutes, but he did not slap them. As he turned towards the POWs I thought he was about to vent his displeasure on us but to my surprise all he said was, "No train, walk camp, I lead, you follow." Handing his bicycle to one of the guards to push, off he went on foot and the rest of us shuffled along behind him. We moved through a number of unpaved streets before reaching the road leading out of town. Most of the buildings we passed seemed to have survived with only minor damage, except in a thoroughfare lined with what looked like warehouses. There nearly all the buildings on the left-hand side leaned backwards at an angle of some 30 degrees. When we reached the main road we found that its concrete surface had cracks running across it. Most of them were only between 3 and 6 inches wide but

154

occasionally we came to one that was over 18 inches across and in those cases one side of the fissure was always raised above the other. These, together with downed telegraph poles and lines, impeded our already slow progress so that it took three and a half hours to complete our journey. By the time we reached camp it was dark and the camp staff were using lanterns for illumination. They did the quickest head count I can remember and dismissed us with none of the usual annoyances. We sloped off into the huts exhausted by the unusual demand on our energy supply.

Power came on in camp the next morning but we did not return to the factory for three days by which time the rail service had been restored. When we reached Nagoya it was noticeable that a number of tracks had been relayed but other than that no other evidence of damage was visible. In the factory things appeared to have returned to normal and machinery was running again, but something seemed different. We all felt it and it became clear that the old zest was missing and the workforce was displaying a much more relaxed attitude. There was a subtle change in their attitude towards us. Perhaps they felt they had lost face having shown that they were just as capable of being scared as we were, or perhaps it was the fact that the earthquake had occurred on the third anniversary of Japan's entry into the war and was therefore a bad omen. I do not know what it was but from that day on not only did their attitude to us change, but it seemed that their morale began to sag and the zeal for work they had hitherto displayed melted away. So much so that the two

155

locomotives in the assembly shop that fell on their side in the earthquake were still lying where they fell when we left for Toyama five months later.

Notes:
1. Shinto is an animistic belief system involving the worship of spirits called Kami. These may be found in a particular place or object such as a stream or a rock. They appear to have a kind of pecking order with the most senior kami relating to major natural objects such as Mount Fuji. The most senior of all is the kami of the Sun Goddess Amaterasu from whom the Emperors of Japan are alleged to descend and are therefore themselves Gods.

   As a religion it seems to concentrate more on the present than the hereafter. It requires the living of a simple and harmonious life with nature and people which is said to involve conforming to the "Four Affirmations", which are:

   (1) Tradition and the family.
   (2) Love of Nature (natural objects containing sacred kami are worshipped).
   (3) Physical cleanliness.
   (4) Celebration of any festival dedicated to kami.

   In 1946, under American pressure, the Emperor renounced his divine status and Shinto ceased to be Japan's state religion. It nevertheless remains the most popular religion in Japan.

CHAPTER
THIRTEEN

On Bombing and Barbarism

To be bombed by your own side is just as frightening as being bombed by the enemy, but in certain circumstances it can also be uplifting. These contradictory emotions surfaced on two of the three occasions when we were on the receiving end of Allied air attacks. During the second and third attack we escaped death by the narrowest of margins, but although scared we were also elated for the attacks meant that Allied forces were getting closer and closer.

It was different on the first the time we saw the insignia of the American Air Force. It was early in our second year at Sham Shui Po and on that occasion we were treated to a relatively safe ringside seat. On the western side of the camp and separated from it by a narrow strip of water was an oil and gasoline storage depot. It comprised twenty large cylindrical tanks spread over an area of about 14 acres with a loading dock on the seaward side. Small coastal tankers used to call in spasmodically and discharged their cargo. It is possible that word of these visits may have been reported to Allied headquarters in Chungking by Nationalist or Communist agents in the Colony for a day after one such visit when a tanker had pumped all the oil it had brought into the tank farm, the Allies struck. They came in the form of a squadron of small fighter-bombers, possibly P-39 Airacobras, in a low-level attack on the oil depot. Diving in from over the hills between the Lion and Amah rocks to the north of the camp, the aircraft flew in line astern, so low that the pilots' heads could be seen inside the canopies and small bombs could be seen falling. Having dropped their bomb load the planes shot out over the harbour, climbed, circled round and dived in for a second run, this time firing their machine guns or cannon at anything that was not already on fire. Then they pulled away and were lost from sight beyond the hills, leaving behind blazing oil tanks that emitted a black pall of smoke that hung over the city for a week. The whole attack probably lasted for no more than five minutes but the sight of those planes with the white stars on their wings and fuselages heartened us for weeks for they were tangible evidence that our side was hitting back.

During that attack we were never in danger of being hit, and could stand and watch the show, but it was not so when the next incident occurred as we were the target. It happened in early January 1945 when we were in Narumi and isolated American aircraft, flying at great height, had been seen from time to time. We spotted one as we climbed the road up to camp on returning from a day in the factory. Inside camp we went through the usual return-to-camp routine and were just entering the huts when there was a whooshing sound rapidly followed by several very loud explosions.

158

The bombs fell just outside the stockade and as the camp was perched right on the top of a hill the main force of the explosions was deflected away from us. The only casualty was one of our number who was hit by a piece of the outer stockade fence which was somehow blown into the camp. The pilot of the aircraft had obviously mistaken us for Japanese troops marching into camp and had decided to drop his bombs on us. We were very lucky — if the aircraft had been a thousand feet lower when it released its bombs I don't think that I would be alive to write about the attack. However, once recovered from the shock we were elated for the raid confirmed our growing belief that Allied aircraft were now roaming unchallenged over the skies of Japan. Regrettably we were not entirely correct in that belief as two horrific incidents involving US airmen were soon to demonstrate.

As we marched back up the hill to camp one evening shortly after the raid I felt ill, and my scalp seemed to stretch and contract. By the time camp was reached and numbering started I felt dreadful and apparently collapsed, for the next thing I remember was lying on a tatami in the medical hut with the air force doctor kneeling over me and saying to my friend the naval sick berth attendant, "Both his lungs are full." I had apparently contracted pneumonia which, as my friend said, in my state of health was not a very intelligent thing to do. He comforted me, though, with the information that the very first Red Cross medicines ever permitted into camp by the Japanese had arrived that day. They comprised, he said, three jars, one each

159

of Glauber's Salts, Epsom Salts and Sulfur Thiasol. The first two, of course, were well known and were not much use to us, but the doctor thought the third one, Sulfur Thiasol, a drug he had never come across before, might be something like Sulfanilamide which was known to us as M and B. So I was given these "unknown" pills at the rate of two every four hours, washed down with gallons of water, and within forty-eight hours I was recovering. I have subsequently been told that Sulfur Thiasol was by far the best treatment for pneumonia available at that time. It certainly worked for me for on my fourth day in the medical hut the Japanese duty sergeant declared me fit for "in-camp duty" and had me discharged. Camp duty involved sweeping the dirt floors of the huts and picking up garbage or any chore that the duty admin sergeant could dream up. It so happened that I was doing something in the yard two mornings after I had been discharged when the main gate was opened and in came a van, a curious-looking vehicle with a carbon-monoxide generator the size of a modern electric water heater stuck on its side. The doors were opened and four soldiers emerged pulling a man after them. He was bent over with his hands tied behind him and was dragged across the compound to the small gate leading to the guardhouse. He was a big man and as he was pushed through the gate I recognized the brown jacket he was wearing and the badge on the shoulder. He was an American airman.

Two days later, having been caught by a guard napping in the afternoon when I was supposed to be working, I was escorted to the guardhouse and handed over to the tender mercies of the sergeant of the guard. He kept me waiting there for about twenty minutes before treating me to what I assume was a torrent of verbal abuse and handing out a dozen hefty slaps across the face. An interpreter then told me that the Japs did not care whether I lived or died and sent me out to work in the factory the next day. Whilst in the guardhouse awaiting my fate, I looked for the American airman but could see no sign of him. I knew he had not been sent to join the American POWs and wondered where he was. Several days passed with no sign of him but obviously something was going on for the guards were more animated than usual and "the Bastard" made an unusual number of visits to the guardroom. Eventually the cookhouse personnel, who could often coax information from the guards, learned that he had been stuffed into a bamboo cage in which he could neither stand up nor sit up as it was only about 4 feet by 3 feet by 2 feet. The cage was kept out of everybody's sight at the back of the guardhouse and he was never let out. He was fed only two tablespoons of rice and two of water a day, the guards came to the cookhouse to collect this ration and it was from them the cooks learned of his fate. They discovered that the guards ran a sweepstake on how long the captive airman would survive, and that he died on the twenty-seventh day. Two weeks after his death another US airman was dragged in and afforded the same treatment. It was reported that he lasted only twenty-three days. This torture of American airmen was sheer barbarism and the frightening thing was that the

161

guards in general, and "the Bastard" in particular, seemed to revel in it.

The next time we came under air attack was in Toyama in the very last month of the war. We knew by then that the American Air Force was systematically bombing major Japanese towns because the Jap newspapers we were able to procure reported the raids. They also referred to a new large aircraft, the B ni jew qu, which had carried out massive fire raids on Tokyo, Yokohama and other large cities, and which very unsportingly flew above the operational ceiling of Japan's defensive fighter aircraft. We did not know then that it was the capture of Pacific islands such as Saipan and Iwo Jima which made the B29 raids possible, but it was a fair assumption that if massive attacks by land planes were being mounted the Allies must be closing in on Japan and the end could not be far away. In this optimistic mood it did not occur to us that Toyama was a potential target for it was, as far as we could see, a small town and, being situated on Japan's west coast, was far distant from the major cities on the east coast that were being attacked. Obviously the Allied planners had different views for at 2.00 a.m. on the morning of 11 August, air-raid warnings were sounded by the blowing of a bugle, and the Japanese drove us all out to sit cross-legged in the middle of the compound. They, on the other hand, sat with machine guns trained on us at the entrances to air-raid shelters they had recently constructed.

We did not have long to wait before we heard the rumble of approaching aircraft. When we saw them they were huge four-engined machines much larger than any aircraft any of us had ever seen and we guessed that they must be the feared B ni jew qu's. They were flying in echelon formation with their wing lights on and at a relatively low altitude. There was no Japanese opposition, not even an anti-aircraft gun. The first wave started dropping its bombs on the far side of the town from the camp. The B29s flew on a steady course during the bombing run before turning left and climbing away. Succeeding waves did the same except that each one seemed to move closer to us. It was as if they were mowing a lawn strip by strip but without turning and doing the reciprocal runs. The attack was well organized for as the last plane of one wave turned and climbed away, the first B29 of the next wave started its run and each one came closer and closer to where we sat. We were between a rock and a hard place for if we moved the Japs would machine gun us and if we sat still it seemed inevitable that firebombs would rain down on us. By the time the attacking aircraft were over the centre of the town the fires started by their predecessors had created a firestorm. It was sucking in so much air that it caused strong sand-laden wind to sweep across the compound where we were sitting, stinging our faces.

As the waves of B29s passed over Toyama they were an awesome sight and even though we knew we were watching what might be the instruments of our own destruction it was impossible to take our eyes off them. I sat mesmerized, as these leviathans of the air seemed to float above the flames, their undersides bathed in the reddish yellow light of the fires. They flew so low that the opening of the huge bomb bay doors could clearly be seen and from the cavernous bellies of the aircraft, large canisters were disgorged. These exploded as they fell releasing a shower of incendiary bombs. I lost count of how many waves of aircraft had passed over the town but by the time it looked as if the next one would pass over us we were all, to say the least, apprehensive. As the leading aircraft of that next wave began its bombing run it seemed that we must be in its path, but by the time it drew level with our position it was about a hundred yards off to one side, with each following aircraft in the echelon a little further over. As the last plane of that wave turned away, with a sinking feeling in the stomach we braced ourselves for the next one. This surely would be the one that would get us. A minute passed and the next wave had not appeared; two minutes passed and then three with still no sign of them. Not daring to believe that the raid had ended we spent some fifteen anxious minutes straining to hear any sound of approaching aircraft, but all we heard was the roar of the wind and an occasional loud crackle from the fires.

Nobody said anything, not even the Japs, but gradually we permitted ourselves to accept that the raid was over. With that acceptance came a wave of elation, partly I suppose as a reaction to fear, but also because we realized that if the Allies could mount raids such as we had just experienced they could not be far away. "The Bastard's" reaction was rather different from ours. Throughout the raid he had stood at the entrance to a shelter with a murderous look on his face. Now it was over he suddenly rushed out into the middle of the compound and ranted at us in Japanese for a good ten minutes before going round kicking everybody as they sat cross-legged on the ground. He then stormed off and that was the last time we ever saw him. It was left to the Sergeant of the Guard to dismiss us. Nobody slept much during what was left of the night — we were too busy wondering what would happen next. Had the factory survived? How close were the Americans? When would they invade?[1] The next few days provided answers to all these questions.

Note:

1. The US Marine commandos, who were the first ground troops to reach us after the surrender, told us that two days after the B29 raid on Toyama, another raid was launched on the town. Its mission was to "destroy everything left standing" and was undertaken by carrier-based aircraft. When it was less than 200 miles from its target the order came to abort — the Japanese had surrendered! In boxing parlance, we had literally been saved by the bell.

    At that time we were still blissfully unaware that in the camp office, as it was in every Japanese POW camp office throughout Japan and Japanese-held territory, was a standing order that at the first hint of invasion of the home islands all prisoners of war were to be executed.

CHAPTER
FOURTEEN

On the End Game

Anyone in the world with access to a radio set learned of the Japanese surrender almost as it happened. Unfortunately we had no radio set and so it took this all-important piece of news a little longer to reach us.

Not surprisingly we were kept in camp for the first two days following the B29 raid. On the third day, by which time power had been restored, we expected to be sent out for even if the factory was not functioning, help would be required to clean up whatever kind of mess it was in. We were told, however, that "there are problems at the factory" and so we stayed put that day and for the next week or so. Then when things seemed to be getting back to normal we were lined up and marched out of camp en route, it was assumed, for the "kaisha". When we were about 200 yards down the lane and had almost reached what had once been "the built-up area", one of the Jap administrative staff came running up and we were halted. We were left standing there for twenty minutes or so and then ordered back to camp.

Whilst we were standing around we had our first opportunity to see the damage inflicted by the raid. The

166

desolation was awful and I was reminded of a scene in a classic 1930s film entitled *The Petrified Forest*. There were no buildings standing, just acres of blackened ground out of which incongruous brick chimneys seemed to grow just as the fossilized trees had in the film. All the buildings had been burnt to ashes and only the incombustible brick chimneys remained. Low-lying wisps of smoke were still visible and the acrid smell of burning lingered in the air. It was a terrible scene. There was no green vegetation visible, no trees, no birds, no sound, no colour except black. It had the appearance of a dead world and I could not help feeling sorry for the people of Toyama, so many of whom must have died.

The following day we went through the same performance except that we were halted just outside the camp gates and stood there looking in. To our amazement we saw two large loudspeakers being set up, one at each end of the compound. A little later the Sergeant Major, a dozen soldiers and one of the Japanese administrative staff came out, all spruced up in what looked like their best uniforms, and gathered round the loudspeakers. After a while a crackling sound came from the speakers followed by a man's voice, then there was a pause followed by martial music and another harsher voice which sounded as if it was barking orders. A gong sounded, all the Japanese bowed deeply and stayed bowed whilst a quiet voice droned on for a few minutes. When it stopped the broadcast was apparently over and the Japs stood up. The privates began asking the Sergeant Major questions but he waved them away and shouted instructions to the guards standing at the entrance gates with us to bring us back into camp where we were promptly dismissed.

Although we did not realize it at the time, the pantomime we had just witnessed was a pivotal event in Japanese history. For centuries Japanese emperors had been revered as gods remote from their subjects who were not worthy to look upon their faces or hear them speak. Their edicts were handed down through courtiers of the highest rank, and they were infallible. A Japanese owed his Emperor not only absolute loyalty but also his life; what we had just been privy to was the momentous occasion when a Japanese Emperor gave up the pretence that he was a god and for the first time ever spoke directly to his people, albeit by radio. His was the last voice we heard coming from the loudspeakers and he was telling his subjects that he had decided to end the war. However, it did not end for us at that moment, but the curious goings on spawned a wave of optimism and speculation. For the two days following the broadcast incident we were kept in camp and whilst most of us felt that the end was near, there was no hard evidence to prove it except possibly that there had been no more air raids. Even that did not count for much for there was very little left to raid. On the third day, however, things began to happen, the rice ration was increased and then we noticed that there were no guards on the gate. That evening the Japanese Sergeant Major called on the senior non-commissioned officer in camp, a warrant officer in the Hong Kong Volunteers, who throughout our time in Japan had had the unenviable task of dealing with the Japanese camp authorities; after the meeting we were told to assemble in the compound. When we did the Japanese Sergeant Major stood up on a box and addressed us. He was quite alone, all the guards had disappeared and "the Bastard" had long since gone. On reflection one cannot but admire the man's courage for what he said in excellent English was, "Gentlemen, the war is over, you will soon be going home." Pandemonium broke out; we were all shouting and laughing at the same time. When we at last quietened down the Japanese spoke again and said, "For your own safety I advise you to remain in camp for the time being."

The next day brought the first example of many we were to experience of Japanese volte-face. It was announced, again by the Sergeant Major, who was the only Japanese left in camp, that the management of the factory where we had been "employed" would like to thank us for our efforts and show their appreciation by providing us with a feast that evening. Sure enough, around six o'clock, men arrived and set up long trestle tables and benches in the compound where a couple of weeks before we had sat cross legged under the muzzles of Japanese machine guns. White cloths were spread over the tables and knives and forks appeared like magic. (The ones that some chaps had carried with them from Hong Kong had been confiscated when we were searched on arrival at Narumi. Anyone who managed to hide his and was subsequently caught with them in a surprise search suffered a nasty beating and a day or more in the guardhouse without food or water.)

169

When we were all sat down a speech was made by a gentleman whom we were told was the company "head man". In reasonably good English he thanked us for our help, said the company had done everything it could to make our stay as pleasant as possible and to safeguard our health. He then wished us a good trip home and good health in the future. When none of the guests moved to reply white china plates were placed in front of us and a dozen or so Japanese men, all dressed in black, served the food. It consisted of white rice, a vegetable that if I remember correctly was daikon, and a steak. It was, I suppose, a noble effort but even though it was the first piece of red meat I had seen in nearly four years I failed to appreciate it. I suspect that an old water buffalo had been killed and butchered to obtain the steak for it was as tough as leather and as I had developed a badly decayed molar tooth chewing it was agony.

In the days following the feast we wandered out of camp to see if there was any way we could communicate with Allied forces but found none. One of our number found what he thought was an alcoholic beverage and partook of it — it was alcohol all right, but wood alcohol and poisonous. When he was found he was unconscious and although still alive when brought back to camp, the doctor could not save him. He died on the third evening of our release. To have survived nearly four years of malnutrition and abuse, and then to die in this manner at that moment seemed a cruel twist of fate. The incident increased our impatience to get out of the country, but we could not find any means of doing so without help. We thought we saw it coming in the afternoon of the fourth day when several small aircraft flew over. They seemed to be flying in a pattern that suggested they were looking for something, but apparently it was not us for even though they flew directly overhead and we waved and waved they flew on. The next day they came again and although they flew all round us they still did not see us and started to fly away, but then I remembered seeing a mirror in the guardroom. I ran in, snatched it off the wall and started to reflect the sun at the departing aircraft. Nothing happened for a moment and then the very last plane in the formation peeled away and flew straight down on us. It roared across the compound as we waved furiously at it and then they all came down. As they crossed the compound they rolled upside down, opened their canopies and dropped whatever was in the crew's pockets. Sticks of chewing gum, opened packets of cigarettes, book matches and even a couple of magazines stamped "USS *Bonadventure*" rained down. It was a very happy moment and I do not know why so many of us could not prevent tears running down our cheeks.

A squadron of Grumman Avengers from the aircraft carrier USS *Bonadventure* visited us the next day and released two small white parachutes attached to which was a wooden box containing in one case medical supplies and in the other tins of meat. A third small red parachute was then dropped and on it was a message tube containing a note that said B29s would be over the next day to drop supplies. When it was clear that we

171

had the message all the aircraft flew low over the compound tossing out cartons of cigarettes and bundles of magazines stamped "Bonadventure Wardroom". This was great stuff and we cheered and waved at every plane as it swept over, but our joy was short lived for one aircraft flew too low and caught its wing tip on the flag pole at the edge of the compound. To our horror it rolled slowly over and crashed into the ground upside down. Mercifully there was no fire but although one crew member was pulled out unharmed and another with only minor injuries, the young nineteen-year-old ensign who had been flying the plane was killed.

This accident took the edge off our high spirits for a while but they recovered three days later when the B29s arrived — bad weather had delayed the much-anticipated arrival — and started dropping supplies. I suppose it was the same aircraft that had bombed Toyama just over a week before. At least they looked the same, flew just as low, you could see the huge bomb doors open and large canisters fall out. I was diving for cover until I realized that the canisters, which on close inspection turned out to be two oil drums welded together end to end, were attached to huge multi-coloured parachutes. They floated down all around the camp, landing mostly in paddy fields and local help, including two venerable water buffalo, was enlisted to retrieve them. When the drums were opened they were found to contain a treasure trove of good things. There were tins of roast beef, ham, lamb stew, bacon, corned beef, sausages, butter, fruits and vegetables. There were cartons of cigarettes and chocolates and for the first time in nearly four years we were able not only to eat our fill but also to do so with Western foods. We were in seventh heaven and perhaps the greatest joy of all at that time was waking up. Whilst asleep, one's subconscious put one back in the prison camp, and so on waking up it took several seconds before the fact that the war over and one was no longer a prisoner registered on the mind. When it did, the relief was profound and the happiness immense. Every night whilst we remained in Toyama I dreamt I was back in the prison camp and throughout my life this dream has persisted. For the first two years after the war it occurred almost once a week but as time passed the frequency diminished. Even now, although it is over a half century since my release, a year does not pass without the dream reoccurring at least once and I awake, perhaps not to the euphoria of earlier years, but sweating and with an immense feeling of relief.

A few days after the B29 visitations (they came over twice) a group of five US Marines flew into the area, and with their help and that of the Japanese Sergeant Major who stayed with us to the very end, a train was organized to take us to the east coast where the Marines told us help awaited.

CHAPTER
FIFTEEN

On the Way Home

After several stops and starts the train deposited us on the east coast of Japan some 200 miles south of Tokyo at a place called Suva Bay. At least that is what we were told was its name, although I have never been able to find such a place on a map. There waiting for us were US sailors with landing craft in which they transported us out to a hospital ship anchored offshore. Once on board we were asked to deposit any souvenirs we wanted to keep in a box and then strip off everything we were wearing. Orderlies in white gowns and wearing masks then sprayed white powder over every part of our anatomy where hair grew before helping us through a bank of showers where we were soaped all over, rinsed off and then handed a luxurious, huge, clean, white towel with which to dry ourselves. Back in civilization at last, I thought, feeling really clean and lice free for the first time in months.

Once out of the showers we came under the scrutiny of a team of doctors who made "travel-or-stay" selections. The lucky ones, like me, were permitted to proceed, while orderlies carted off the others to the ship's hospital wards. Of the 170 or so of us who had

174

survived to this point out of the 300 who left Hong Kong, ninety were deemed fit to travel; the rest were confined to a hospital bed. From the "selection room" we proceeded to the kitting-out store where with help from a number of enthusiastic quartermasters we emerged in all the finery the US provides for its service personnel. Fitting had been a bit of a problem as none of us had a normal anatomical shape. In my case, for example, I had been weighed before entering the selection room, and despite eating all the goodies the B29s had supplied, I still only turned the scale to 105lb. As I had weighed 164lb in December 1941, like the rest of my fellow prisoners, I had shrunk somewhat and the poor quartermasters must have felt that they were trying to outfit a bunch of skeletons, which I suppose we were.

From the kitting-out store we were led to the communications centre where we were assisted in sending telegrams to our relatives. The Americans had everything well organized — all one had to do was supply a name and address, and choose one of a number of standard messages. I cabled my parents in England: "Safe and well in Allied hands. Hope to see you soon. Send mail c/o Repatriated POWs Base Post Office, Melbourne, Australia." In the event we did not go anywhere near Australia but at the time it was thought that was where all UK repatriates would be sent.

With the clothing and communications matters dealt with we were plied with food and cigarettes, with chocolates and chewing gum, and something we had never seen before, paperback books. The crew could not do enough for us and whilst an orderly painted my decayed tooth to numb the pain, he said he was terribly sorry that there were no dentists on board who could fix the problem. He told me, however, that there were bound to be dental facilities available when we reached a shore base and that we would be leaving for Yokohama shortly. We left the hospital ship the evening of the same day that we boarded her. Three destroyers came alongside one after the other and thirty of us were embarked on each of them. Like the hospital ship crew, those on the destroyers did everything they could to make us feel comfortable. They cheerfully gave up their bunks to us and told us there was a special welcome waiting for us in Tokyo Bay where the grand fleet was assembled.

We reached the Bay on a beautiful sunny morning and there stretched out as far as the eye could see were endless lines of warships. A British Battleaxe-class destroyer came out to meet us and then lead the three destroyers in line astern between the lines of massive capital ships, which comprised the core of the vast armada. The decks of the huge battleships were lined with cheering sailors and as we moved down the lines it was the same as we passed aircraft carriers, cruisers and smaller ships. It was a very emotional moment and I do not think there was a dry eye among us. Even now, more than a half century later, I cannot recall that moment without feeling again something of the tug on the heartstrings that brought tears to our eyes on that late August morning in 1945.

Eventually we left the fleet and proceeded into Yokohama harbour where we tied up alongside a tank landing craft. We paused there just long enough for some more painkillers to be applied to my tooth before being trucked out to the Japanese Naval Air Station at Atzuki near Tokyo. From there it was the intention to fly us straight out to Okinawa en route for Manila in the Philippines, but bad weather closed the airport. As the American forces had only moved in two days before our arrival I anticipated that we were in for a long uncomfortable night, but in fact it was anything but uncomfortable. Camp beds by the hundred had already been set up in one hanger and the one next door had been turned into a huge PBX store. It was stocked with an unimaginable wealth of goodies from toilet items to cigarettes, from underwear to chocolates, and from patent medicines to chewing gum, and we were constantly encouraged to go and help ourselves. I looked at the tempting array, and thought that just a month earlier some of those things would have been worth their weight in gold and would have brought us great delight. Now that they were available in abundance and I was well fed, however, I could not bring myself to take anything except for some cigarettes.

By the morning the weather had cleared and flying recommenced. I was loaded on to a civilian airliner and flown to Okinawa. There we met up with other POWs and were housed in a tented camp. At seven o'clock in the morning of the day after our arrival my name was called over the public address system instructing me to

177

report to the guardroom at eight o'clock. When I did I was told that I was about to have my tooth fixed, although how the people in Okinawa knew I had a bad tooth I do not know for I had not mentioned it to anyone since my arrival. Anyway, after a few minutes wait in the guardroom, I heard a deafening roar and saw a helicopter land in the small square outside. "Right, off we go," said a medical sergeant and lead me and two other repats out of the door and into the helicopter, which promptly took off. The flight lasted about twenty-five minutes and we landed at a field hospital where, among other things, were four dentist's chairs and associated equipment under thatched roofs. I was consigned to one of them where a US Army dentist set about examining my teeth. He was a man in his late thirties who told me that he had been called up for military service and inevitably been assigned to the Dental Corps. His examination was thorough and relatively painless. He asked how long I had been a prisoner and what kind of food we had had. He then said, "I am very sorry but I am afraid that I will have to take that decayed tooth out. Had we been in the States and I had all my equipment I might have been able to save it, but I cannot do it here nor can I let you proceed with the condition it is in." So he removed the offending tooth, the first of my adult teeth to go, but I consoled myself with the thought that it could have been a lot worse — he could have said all my teeth were in a poor condition. He did not say that but instead took me into the mess and fed me ice cream and soft drinks once the numbness from the anesthetic began to wear off. From him I learned about the dropping of the atomic bombs and how they had expedited the end of the war,[1] and that there was a new crooner on the scene who challenged the dominance of Bing Crosby — "A young skinny kid called Frank Sinatra."

On the flight back to camp the pilot insisted on giving us a tour of the island, pointing out the spots where the most intense fighting had taken place. As a result I did not get back to my friends until early evening, to discover that we were already on notice to depart at seven the next morning en route for Manila. Trucks took us to the airfield where we were loaded, ten at a time, into B17 bombers! Six-inch-wide planks had been placed over the bomb racks on both sides of the aircraft. So we sat five on each rack facing each other, trying to make our feet as comfortable as possible on the 6-inch catwalk that separated us. Some 4 inches below the catwalk were the bomb bay doors and through the small gap between them the ground was visible less than a foot below. Fortunately we were only confined to these uncomfortable and noisy seating arrangements during landing and take-off. Once the aircraft reached cruising altitude the captain told us to move around and invited us up to the cockpit to try our hand at flying the plane. I was one who tried, much to the chagrin of my fellow repats who claimed, admittedly with some justification, that I flew it in such an erratic manner that they were airsick. We were herded back into the bomb bay as we approached Clark Field in Manila and there was a moment of panic when the engineer came rushing back aft to peer out of what normally would have been the air gunner's windows. As he returned he explained that a report from the ground said that one B17 had an engine fire and he had gone aft to ensure that it was not us. Fortunately it was not and we landed uneventfully, provided one overlooked the fact that one was suspended on a 1-inch plank over empty bomb racks watching the runway flash past at 150 miles an hour 12 inches below one's cramped feet! We all thanked the crew for the ride and as we walked away a senior officer approached them. I heard him say to the captain, "Your crate is being refueled. I'll give you twenty minutes before you take off and start back to wherever the hell you came from."

Leaving the crew to their coffee break we boarded buses and were driven to a huge camp just outside Manila where all ex-POWs were being assembled. It was here that I met some of the people who been kept in Hong Kong, including the old boys from the boom defence vessel. They were as glad to see me as I was them and they told me how the Sham Shui Po camp had gradually been reduced in size until in the end it comprised just the Jubilee buildings and a dozen or so huts. When Royal Navy ships entered port they had ventured out and found the town in pretty poor shape. Nevertheless, they had managed to scrounge foodstuffs, clothing and blankets from the arriving forces and took them to their old girlfriends before leaving for Manila, where they arrived a few days ahead of us. As in the past, they had the most reliable information on what was happening, and told us that a British aircraft carrier was being sent to collect us and transport us back to England. We were not going to Australia as was originally announced and the aircraft carrier was due in Manila by the end of the week. As always though, there was a dissenting voice among them who thought that knowing the way the Navy worked "we would be bloody lucky to see an aircraft carrier this side of Christmas."

It certainly did not arrive by the weekend and we began to envy the American ex-POWs who were being shipped out to the States every day. In retrospect it seems ridiculous that after what we had been through a few days waiting for transport should make us so impatient to be on the move again, but such was the case. I suppose that since leaving Toyama we had been moved along so rapidly that we had begun to expect instant action. Our hosts, the US Army, did their best to keep us entertained, even to the extent of bussing us in to see the ruins that had once been the thriving city of Manila. It was a most depressing sight having been the scene of bitter house-to-house fighting between US and Japanese forces.

After nearly a week in the Manila camp there came a surprising announcement by the US commander, who announced over the public address system that "as from tomorrow all ships leaving Manila for the States will carry fifty per cent US ex-POWs and fifty per cent UK ex-POWs." Within twenty-four hours, in company with a thousand US and a thousand UK ex-POWs, I was embarked on an American troopship, the USS *Admiral Hughes*, and commenced the 21-day eastward crossing of the Pacific. It was a very pleasant voyage

181

with nothing to do except eat, drink, smoke, talk, play cards and watch the movies shown every night in the mess hall, with the comforting thought at the back of one's mind that every turn of the ship's propellers took us nearer home. Two things happened though on that voyage that have stuck in my mind and to an extent influenced what I was to do in later life.

As part of the ship's entertainment programme there was a "questions box" on the upper deck into which all ex-POWs were encouraged to place written questions on any subject they liked. At five o'clock each evening the question and its answer would be read out by an announcer over the public address system. The standard of questioning was not high with more interest being shown in the essential measurements of the nurses in the sick bay than in world affairs. However one evening, when we had been at sea for a week, the announcer came on as usual at five o'clock and stated that a very important question had been asked and the Commanding Officer had decided to answer it himself. The question was from a US ex-POW who wanted to know "Why is it that this ship is carrying fifty per cent Limey ex-POWs when lots of my buddies are left on the beach in Manila?" The CO's answer made me look up and take notice. He said, "The UK was in the war fighting for freedom and liberty two and a quarter years before we got into it and for much of that time it was fighting alone. Therefore if there was any real equity in this world this ship would be carrying one hundred per cent UK ex-POWs and the questioner would still be on the beach with the rest of his buddies."

182

More was to come for the very next day he fell in all the US ex-POWs and paid them US$40 each. He then turned to the old British Army Brigadier who had been sent out from the UK to oversee our passage home and said, "Now you had better pay your chaps." That unfortunate elderly gentleman, who had seen service in the First World War, and possibly the Boer War before that, had no authority to pay anybody, and in any event, at that time England was right out of dollars. On learning this the US commander decided it was a bad thing that half his charges should have money and the other half should not, so he fell us in and paid us all twenty dollars each. I have often wondered how he explained to government auditors why he paid out US$20,000 to foreign troops, especially when there was nothing on which to spend it. But pay us he did and in so doing probably sowed the seed in my mind that one day I must visit the land which produced this larger-than-life character whose name I never discovered (of course thirty years later I did and became an American citizen).

Right on schedule, three weeks after leaving Manila we arrived at Esquimalt, the naval port near Victoria in British Columbia, Canada. There were bands and crowds to meet us but we were whisked rapidly away to an adjacent military barracks. There we were kept virtually in seclusion for two days whilst we were subject to thorough medical examinations and asked to provide details of any atrocities that we had witnessed whilst prisoners. Not even the press was allowed into the barracks whilst these proceedings were taking place.

183

In the evening of the second day, however, we were all assembled and the Canadian authorities apologized for detaining us, but deemed it necessary to ensure that any information that might be of use in war crimes trials was extracted from us and passed to the appropriate agencies before the press got at us. They also said that the medical examinations had revealed that although most of us were fit enough to proceed on our way home, there were a few who had needed immediate hospitalization. As to the next move, the UK government had informed them it would not be possible to have a ship available to take us home from the east coast port of Halifax for another three weeks. We therefore had a choice. We could proceed overland by rail immediately to Halifax and wait there. As the rail journey would take a week, that meant we would be in Halifax, or more precisely at the De Bert military camp a few miles outside that town, for two weeks. Alternatively, we could stay in Victoria for two weeks and then proceed across the country. The latter choice was recommended because the good citizens of Victoria, anxious to repay some of the hospitality afforded their sons in England, wanted to take us into their homes and give us a taste of civilian life before we returned home. It was thought that this would do us much more good than twiddling our thumbs in an army camp on the other side of the continent. We were given until the morning to make our individual decisions, but in the event it was made for us. The gates of the camp were thrown open at nine o'clock and hundreds of cars streamed through — half of Victoria must have been there. We were literally picked up, driven into town and shown the sights. Together with another Navy type I stayed for two weeks with a retired farmer and his wife and family. When they took us into town to a restaurant, the proprietor refused to give us a bill. The prestigious Canadian Pacific Hotel offered us the use of its swimming pool and everybody did their best to make us feel welcome. Victoria and its environs are one of the most beautiful parts of Canada. We all enjoyed our stay there and it is a source of great satisfaction to me that although the farmer and his wife have long since died I still remain in contact with their children.

In a way those good people of Victoria gave us more than they realized. We had been too long away from polite society and when we first entered their civilian homes we were tongue-tied. Everyone I spoke to had the same experience. We had lost the art of normal conversation and all felt terribly shy. As the days passed we began to relax and became more comfortable in what was for us new and unusual circumstances, but when they first had us in their homes our hosts must have thought us a little strange. Very much to their credit, though, they gave no sign that they found us anything but normal and by so doing built up our self-confidence, so that we were in much better shape for our homecoming than we would have been had we not spent those two weeks rehabilitation in the floral capital of western Canada.

Whilst we were in Victoria most people received messages from their families in England but as I did not, and as my people lived in Southampton which had been heavily bombed and had been the target for V1 and V2 rockets, I became concerned. In desperation I sent a telegram to my uncle who lived in the country and his reply arrived the day before we left Victoria. Very much to my relief I learned that my parents, brother and sister were fine but they had moved to a new address — for some unknown reason my communications had not been forwarded on to them. So with the last and most awful fear of my years as a POW put to rest, I set out on the penultimate leg of the long journey home in fine spirits.

The rail journey across Canada took five days and six nights. The first part through the Rockies was fascinating. I saw some of the most magnificent scenery I have ever seen on that part of the journey, but as we moved out onto the prairies the view from the train windows was less attractive. It was all the same flat land covered for the most part with wheat fields and the view in the morning was the same as that when we had gone to bed. Eventually though we reached Toronto where thousands turned out to meet the train, then on just south of Montreal and through part of Maine to Halifax. Fortunately the ship that was to take us home, the *Ile de France*, had already arrived and so we went straight aboard. She sailed that evening and five days later we were off the Isle of Wight stuck in a fog. We had been due to dock in Southampton docks at 10.00 a.m. but that found us inching our way up the Solent. Another hour passed and I thought we were never going to get home when suddenly the fog cleared and there before us were the ocean docks lined with people. As tugs gently manoeuvred the ship into her berth I saw my mother, father, younger brother and sister in the crowd. It was five years since I had seen them, my siblings had grown and my parents aged. I suppose I had too but they recognized me and were waving furiously. I knew that I was home and my long journey was over.

Note:

1. Over the years since the war whenever someone discovered that I had been a POW in Japan they nearly all asked the same question: "Were you anywhere near where the atomic bombs were dropped?" They showed far more interest in the atomic bombs and the devastation they caused than in the prison camps. Fortunately I was not in a position to provide any first-hand information for it was not until we had left Japan that we learned that the bombs had been dropped. After the big fire raid on Toyama and in the excitement of being free, very little news had reached the camp. There were no newspapers to steal and with no electric power to run the Jap radio sets we found (even if we could repair them after the departing guards had attempted to destroy them before they left), the only outside news we received came from the Japanese Sergeant Major who stayed with us to the very end. He had said that two very large bombs had been dropped, one on Hiroshima and one on Nagasaki (both of which are a long way from Toyama) and

that many people had been killed. He also said he thought the Emperor, who alone had the power to do so, must have decided to surrender the country in order to avoid further loss of civilian life. It was not until we were aboard the hospital ship that we learned that things called atomic bombs had been dropped on two Japanese cities causing tremendous damage and loss of life. We were told that atomic bombs were the size of golf balls and their effect was so devastating that the Japanese were forced to surrender. The Sergeant Major's story proved to be correct but what we were told on the hospital ship was not quite accurate. It was not until some years later that the full story of what happened in those tumultuous days in August 1945 was made public. Apparently the Japanese government had put out feelers through the Russian Embassy to see if peace could be negotiated on better terms than the unconditional surrender called for at the Potsdam conference attended by Churchill, Roosevelt and Stalin. Before even a reply was received Stalin somewhat belatedly fulfilled his promise to the Allies to declare war on Japan once Germany had been defeated. Russian forces entered Mongolia and others captured a group of small Japanese islands far to the north of the Japanese home islands. This raised the possibility that one day those home islands could be attacked from two directions — the Americans from the south and the Russians from the north. Then shortly after the Russians declared war on Japan the two atomic bombs (each of which was nearer the size of a small car than that of a golf ball) were dropped and this was the final straw that brought about the surrender. It was not easily done, however, for the militarists in the government strongly opposed it, and only when the Emperor himself stated the war must be ended and proposed to make the announcement (and thereby take the blame) was the matter decided. Even then a group of young "fight-to-the-death" officers, imbued with the Samurai spirit, endeavoured to stop the announcement being made. The Emperor had recorded his speech on two identical disks, one copy of which was to be retained in the Imperial Palace in Tokyo and the other sent to the Government Radio Station for general broadcast on a predetermined day and time, thus allowing the decision to be made known to all important military and government officials before being broadcast to the world. These young officers waylaid the official taking the disk to the radio station and for a while there was an uneasy stand-off between the General responsible for security at the Palace and the rebel group. Everything depended on to whom the Palace guards would give their allegiance. Fortunately they remained loyal to the General and the leader of the young officers was either killed or committed hari-kari (ritual suicide).

In America, the President, Harry Truman, who as Vice-President earlier in the year had succeeded to the Presidency following the untimely death of President Roosevelt, had only learned of the

189

existence of atomic bombs after he became the President. He was told there were only two bombs and it would take at least six months before another could be manufactured. Whilst the bombs were considered ready for use and their effect devastating there was no absolute guarantee that they would function correctly. When used there would inevitably be huge civilian casualties. Because their effect would be so great and large areas might be contaminated with long-term radiation, one group argued that a bomb should be dropped on an uninhabited Japanese island to demonstrate to the Japs its awful destructive power. This argument was refuted by others on the grounds that if the demonstration bomb should fail our position would be weakened rather than enhanced, and it was not a risk we could afford to take. Furthermore, even if the first bomb did not fail we would only have one left with which to drive our point home if the Japanese decided to fight on despite the threat of atomic bombs.

The decision on what course to follow lay entirely with the President and must have been one of the most horrendous decisions any human being has had to make. He argued that the most important objective was to end the war as soon as possible and decided that dropping both bombs on Japanese targets offered the best chance of achieving that result. So he approved the dropping of the two bombs and by so doing brought the war to a close.

He was severely criticized by some in the post-war

years for introducing atomic warfare, and by others for not taking the course advocated by those who had suggested dropping a bomb on an uninhabited island as a demonstration of its powers. This, it is claimed, might have saved the tremendous loss of life whilst still achieving the desired result. On the other hand, of course, it might not and none of his critics were privy to another piece of information that President Truman had in the summer of 1945, but which did not become known to the public until the relevant Top Secret documents were declassified some sixty years later. This was the plan for the invasion of Japan, code-named "Operation Downfall", which was due to commence on 1 November 1945 after the end of the typhoon season. The first landings were to be on Kyushu, the southernmost of the Japanese home islands, followed some six months later in May 1946 by landing on the largest island Honshu, probably in the Tokyo Bay area (see map on page 192-193).

The plan necessitated the use of over one and a half million combat troops, with millions more soldiers in support roles and an armada of over 3,000 ships of all kinds. In view of the magnitude of the task perhaps these numbers are not surprising. What was surprising in the declassified documents was the anticipated strength of the Japanese home-based forces. On Kyushu they were thought to have a large number of elite, highly trained and well-equipped troops. They were expected to put up a fanatical defence of their home territory and

191

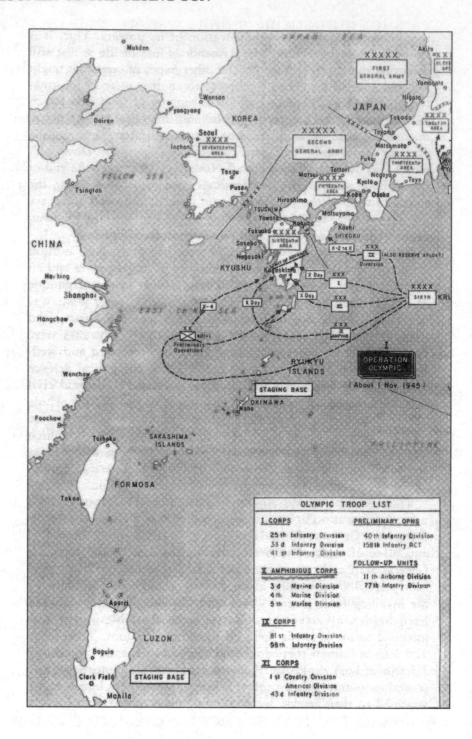

OLYMPIC TROOP LIST

I CORPS

25th Infantry Division
33d Infantry Division
41st Infantry Division

V AMPHIBIOUS CORPS

3d Marine Division
4th Marine Division
5th Marine Division

IX CORPS

81st Infantry Division
98th Infantry Division

XI CORPS

1st Cavalry Division
Americal Division
43d Infantry Division

PRELIMINARY OPNS

40th Infantry Division
158th Infantry RCT

FOLLOW-UP UNITS

11th Airborne Division
77th Infantry Division

OPERATION OLYMPIC

(About 1 Nov. 1945)

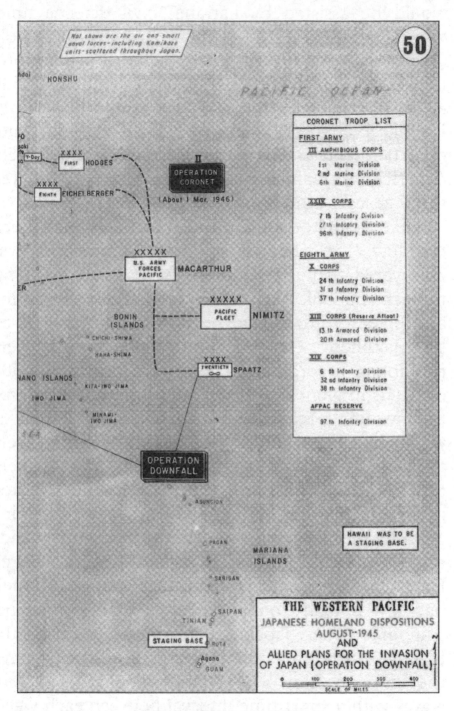

The Western Pacific

would be assisted by national civil defence units which would have the effect of turning the whole country into one huge armed camp. Furthermore, the Japanese were thought to have about 2,500 aircraft available, some of which would be used in Kamikaze attacks. Attacks by human torpedoes and other suicidal devices were also anticipated. American casualties were conservatively estimated to be at least a million.

That estimate would almost certainly have been too low, for when Japan was occupied it was discovered that the Japanese forces there were far more formidable than anticipated. Both the timing and place of attack had been correctly forecast by the Japanese General Staff and troops were positioned accordingly. There were nearly 800,000 on Kyushu alone, so they would have outnumbered the invading force three to two. Over 12,000 planes, which had been hidden all over the country, were available and it was intended to use most of them on Kamikaze missions. There were 120 kaiten human torpedoes that carried warheads containing 1,500lb of high explosive. Four thousand suicide motorboats and several thousand frogmen called Fukuryu, armed with limpet mines strapped to their backs, were ready to make suicidal attacks on enemy shipping. The Japanese planned to use the Kamikaze aircraft as the first line of defence against the invasion fleet. The attacks would be in four waves with a short time interval between each wave, the first and possibly the second of which was expected to be destroyed by the invading fleet's carrier-borne aircraft. The third and forth waves were to be timed so that they arrived over the fleet when the defending aircraft had been forced to withdraw in order to refuel. The principal targets were to be the troop transport ships.

There can be no doubt that President Truman made the right decision.

Epilogue

Adapting to civilian life was not as easy as I had anticipated. The long years in the prison camps had not only been detrimental to one's health but had left the mind out of condition. I found, for example, that mathematics that had once been my forte was no longer so and comprehension of complex concepts was annoyingly difficult. I failed by a narrow margin two professional examinations that I should have passed easily and began to feel frustrated. The post I had had in the civil service, whilst desirable in the days of the pre-war depression for the job security it afforded, was no longer attractive and I suppose I missed the camaraderie that bound all POWs together.

I felt I was becoming depressed and made a conscious effort to remind myself how fortunate I was to be alive. I recalled the number of instances where death had been escaped by a hair's breadth. For example, the bombs that just missed in Narumi, the two paddy fields that saved us in the fire raid on Toyama and the atomic bomb that was dropped on Japan and ended the war without an invasion of the Japanese home islands which would have meant our execution. I thought too that had

I not been sick with diphtheria I would have been on the ill-fated *Lisbon Maru* draft, and then there was the timely arrival of the diphtheria serum in Sham Shui Po and the sulfur thyasol in Narumi. Were these all coincidences or were there other influences at work? My mother thought there were — she had prayed for my safe return every night since I joined the Navy. She told me that twice whilst I was a prisoner she heard me calling to her during the night and as far as I was able to ascertain those two occasions coincided with the times I was ill with diphtheria and pneumonia.

Two years after my release, although my mind was back up to speed, I was still experiencing periods of self-doubt and indecision. I had bought a motorcycle with my Navy back pay and it gave me mobility, which seemed to be something I craved. Riding it around one day with no particular destination in mind I found myself in Salisbury and remembered that according to the Bishop who had confirmed me in the Church of England, this was my home. I had been about eleven years old at the time and although we lived then in Poole in Dorset I was confirmed by the Bishop of Salisbury in whose see my local church was located. I remember him seeing each one of us communicants after the ceremony and having a few words with us. He told me that wherever I went in the world Salisbury would always be my home. The fact that Salisbury, a town I had not then visited, was to be my home did not mean very much at the time. Nor did I feel any sense of homecoming now I was in the town, but I decided that whilst there I might as well visit the magnificent cathedral with its towering spire and its copy of the Magna Carta.

I walked along the path across the extensive lawn that encompasses two sides of the cathedral, marvelling at the dedication and skill of men, dead some 700 years, who had produced this wonderful physical expression of their faith. I felt they must have had stronger faith than that of contemporary Christians. I could not envisage anyone building a new church let alone a cathedral in the social economic climate that prevailed in 1947. Then I came to the outer entrance doors that opened onto a small lobby, at the end of which was another set of doors leading into the cathedral itself. I stepped through and as I did so was enveloped in something which defies description. The best I can do is liken it to being immersed in a hot bath after the first football practice of the season and feeling the aches and the stiffness drain away. Only the relaxation was not of the body but of the mind. Clarity of thought ensued and intensified as I entered the cathedral proper. Things that had been troubling me faded into insignificance and it felt as though my mind was being rearranged into a more efficient configuration. I began to know what I should do and what direction I should take. Quiet confidence replaced my indecision and I was conscious of a deep feeling of well-being. I felt physically liberated and seemed to float around the cathedral. My vision was enhanced as though a film, such as that caused by the cataracts I developed in later life, had been removed from my eyes and everything looked brighter and more colourful. I remained in the cathedral for nearly an hour and the strange and wonderful feeling stayed with me throughout. The moment I stepped outside it was gone just as if it had been switched off. I have been back to Salisbury Cathedral many times and I always felt at home there, but the phenomenon has never reoccurred.

It does not have to for the one experience cleared my mind and showed the way forward. As to what it was, I know it was not an hallucination. My fiancée was with me when I experienced it and I was able to tell her about it as it happened. It could not have been drug induced for other than prescribed medication I have never taken a drug in my life. I believe it came from beyond the dimensional limitations of terrestrial life, from something or some force that for want of a better word most of us refer to as God. For me His (or Hers or Its) existence is no longer in doubt and I have complete faith that He does.

I once told this story to one of my grandchildren when she was very young and had no inhibitions. If I remember correctly she asked, "If you have faith, Grandpa, why don't you go to church more often?" I do not think I gave a satisfactory answer and even now when I ask myself the same question, the answer does not come easily. My thinking has evolved over the years particularly since I retired and to explain my present thoughts I have to review my past churchgoing experience.

When I was a boy I was in the choir at my local church, so on Sundays I had to attend the morning and evening service and go to Sunday school in the afternoon. Choir practice was held on Thursday evenings, and on high days and holidays there were additional church services. The Sunday ritual was well ingrained in me, so much so that when I left home to go to work in Gloucester I automatically went to church on Sunday, although in Gloucester it was not a church I attended, but a Cathedral, a magnificent example of medieval architecture and piety, the kind of building that exudes an almost spiritual atmosphere and a timeless commitment to a belief. It has a sort of magnetic effect that makes me feel that I want to be there. Milton describes it far better than I can in these lines from Il Penseroso:

But let my due feet never fail
To walk the studious cloisters pale,
And love the high-embowed roof,
With antique pillars massy proof,
And storied windows richly dight,
Casting a dim religious light.

At sixteen that building really impressed me and it still does.

This churchgoing habit was broken for me, as it was for multitudes of other people, by the war which did not recognize any difference between Sunday and any other day. So by the time I came home in the autumn of 1945 I had completely lost the habit. I had not forgotten the Church and all the good work it does. I admire its members who have devoted their lives to help others and have endured extreme hardship to bring comfort and help to the sick and the poor. Their compassion and courage sets standards too high for most of us to reach. I still remembered the church music and its festivals and I found myself attending them, but no longer was I a regular churchgoer. As the years passed I kept my faith but began to question religion. Whilst I recognized that it had been a great civilizing influence in the world it also seemed to have been very divisive. I got to thinking of that monastery in Hong Kong where an attempt had been made to establish what I had called an "Esperanto" religion, i.e. an amalgam of the three major world religions. Back then it seemed that it would have a reasonable chance of success. It might be a slight oversimplification to say that all three worshipped the same God, advocated the same code of behaviour and the only difference between them was that they could not agree over who was the true prophet. But surely between men of goodwill, it should not be too difficult to negotiate some kind of modus operandi that would allow them all to live peacefully and co-operatively together.

When I retired and had the time to study the history of religion, I soon realized that only my complete lack of knowledge of the subject had allowed me to think in those simplistic terms. It soon became apparent that the difference I mentioned above had little to do with today's reality. I do not think it is the principal reason for the split between the religions. It may constitute the basic argument and the specific belief put forward by the leaders of religious bodies to distinguish their particular brand of religion and to justify their claim to be the preachers of the only true faith. However, at the time that the three major religions were in their formative years some 2,000 years ago, these differences must have been minimal. Even today the Koran devotes a whole chapter to Jesus, declaring him the most important prophet after Mohammed, and the only one credited with the ability to perform miracles and rise from the dead. I find it very difficult to believe that arguments over who was the true messiah could be the only or indeed the principle reason why three major religions preaching the same basic philosophy arose, when logically one would suffice. I suspect that what really happened was not so much a clash of faiths but a power struggle, because during the first one and a half millennia after the birth of Christ, religious power equated to Political power. The history of the Christian religion amply illustrates this.

Although all the stories in the Christian Bible (and for that matter in the Jewish Torah and Bible, and in the Koran) emanate from the Middle East, Rome became the power base for the largest Christian group, the Catholics. It happened even though Constantine, the first Roman Emperor to convert to the Christian faith, had his capital in Constantinople at the time of his conversion. He was seeking something that would have a unifying influence throughout his disparate Empire. He thought one all-embracing religion instead of the many pagan Gods might be just the thing, and so decreed that the whole Empire must follow his lead and become Christian. When the Roman Emperors returned to Rome the head of the Catholic Church went with them and has remained there to this day.

However, early in the history of the Christian religion, splinter groups broke off and created their own cultural centres, laws and rituals. The historical record as to why and how they broke off is sketchy but now there are six varieties of the Christian faith: Roman Catholic, Greek Orthodox, Armenian Apostolic, Syrian Orthodox, Coptic Orthodox and Ethiopian Orthodox. The fact that there are so many would appear to support the view that it was not dogma or belief that stimulated the multiplicity of religions, but a struggle for power. Even now in the twenty-first century, when religion appears to be on the wane, there is no attempt to merge. Furthermore Christian religious leaders still argue over which group is the rightful custodian of Christianity's most holy shrine, the Church of the Holy Sepulchre in Jerusalem, which is built on the spot where Jesus is believed to have been crucified. Fights broke out between the sects with monotonous regularity right up to the nineteenth century. At that time Jerusalem was part of the Ottoman Empire and in 1852 the Sultan, fed up with having to deal with the sectarian fights, divided the Church into six different territories, awarding one such territory to each of the six claimants, with the doors as common ground. It remains in this state today and six different Orders of Monks still care for their closely guarded section of the church.

The Roman Catholic faith flourished in most of Europe and as a result the Church of Rome had de facto unopposed political power there right up to the end of the seventeenth century. The clergy were very clever in using religious doctrine as a tool with which to manipulate and direct the secular powers. They alone could give a King the spiritual blessing confirming his divine right to rule without which he would not get far. They laid down codes for moral behavior and enforced them with threats of damnation if they were not followed. They influenced the policies of the civil administration and played a direct part in the determination of foreign affairs. In this they had the advantage of what for the time was a sophisticated communication network across the whole of Europe. It was they who invented the Notary Public system, which we still use today, to ensure the authenticity of communications reaching Rome. They also had a spy network that was not equalled until the Communist and Fascist states erupted in the middle of the twentieth century.

The Church had an intriguing financing technique. Churchgoers were expected to confess their sins regularly to a priest who could dispense forgiveness and impose a punishment which might be a form of community service and/or a monetary payment. It also stated that one's place in Heaven could be assured if one made substantial gifts to charity and to the Church. In other words, salvation could be bought. This resulted in vast amounts of wealth being donated to the Church. Whole estates were given to monasteries and abbeys, and bishops began to live in luxurious "bishop's palaces". There is little doubt that this financing technique was what made possible the building of the magnificent cathedrals that are to be found all over Europe today.

The Church was able to impose its will on the people in this way by exploiting their ignorance. It ensured that only the clergy had access to the Holy Scriptures, the most important of which was the Holy Bible. It did this by keeping all its written material within the confines of Church premises and ensuring they were written in Latin, the language in which part of all church services was conducted. Very few people could read in the Church's early days and those who could were unlikely to understand Latin. On the other hand all the clergy were taught that language, so it was they who translated the Holy Word and preached it to the parishioners. They could therefore be selective in what they preached and could emphasize passages that suited their purpose. They could do this far more easily than today's secular governments because no lay person knew what was in the Holy Scriptures so no one could challenge the Church's interpretation.

This happy state of affairs for the Roman Church began to deteriorate during the Middle Ages. Because it refused to sanction a divorce from his first queen, King Henry VIII of England broke with Rome and made himself the head of the Church. He promptly took over all the lands and wealth of the Catholic Church, threw out its clergy and appointed his own. Nevertheless his new Church retained much of the customs and rituals of its predecessor and the same administrative structure, leading up to archbishops who were made members of the House of Lords (and still are). These arrangements with a few minor changes were confirmed at a conference, presided over by Henry's daughter, Elizabeth I, a few years after her fathers' death. It was this conference which brought into being

205

the present-day Church of England (or Episcopalian Church as it is known in America). Not everyone was satisfied with the new organization, Catholicism went underground and radical reformists complained that a more simplistic form of worship was needed. All this was a blow to the Roman Church which reacted by encouraging Catholic countries, particularly Spain, to go to war with the British. The blow was relatively minor, however, compared with what was to come. The real troubles began when the enormous wealth of the Church began to be questioned and one or two brave and brilliant souls had the temerity to translate the Bible into their native language.

Luther did it in Germany, whilst in England first Whitcliff and then Tindale made translations. Whitcliff's Bible preceded the printing press and copies of it were hand written, but by the time Tindale completed his translation printing was well established. Both men were declared heretics by the religious authorities and had to go into hiding. Tindale managed to cross the Channel to the Belgian port of Antwerp, where any kind of trade could safely be carried on provided it was profitable to the locals. So they gladly printed his Bible and smuggled it into England where it was in great demand. He stayed there incognito for seven years before a paid informant betrayed him and he was taken back to England. There he was tried, declared a heretic and suffered the same punishment as had earlier been imposed on Whitcliff — he was burned at the stake.

His efforts and those of Whitcliff were not in vain for they set in motion revolutionary new thought processes that would shake the Church's very foundations. The two main issues the reformers concentrated on once they had assimilated the Bible's contents were firstly that Jesus' teachings did not demand elaborate and ornate meeting places, and secondly, salvation could not be bought, it could be achieved only by faith. The argument raged over many years. At one point extremists like Cromwell and his Puritans, the Taliban of their day, conquered the whole of England, destroyed much Church and royal property and imposed draconian rules of behaviour. However Cromwell's Commonwealth, as he called it, did not last long and the Monarchy was restored. The son of the King, Charles I, who Cromwell had beheaded, was recalled from exile and crowned Charles II. With the return of the Monarchy, there was a reaction to Cromwell's austere regime and this tended to weaken the standing of the Church. Charles II enjoyed the material pleasures of life but apparently had a hankering for the Catholic faith and converted to Catholicism on his death bed. He had no legitimate heir (although it is claimed that he had eighteen illegitimate ones) so the Crown passed to his brother James, who was a Roman Catholic. So for a short while the incongruous situation existed that the Head of the Church of England was a Roman Catholic! This situation was tolerated whilst he had no male heir but when his second wife, also a Roman Catholic, bore him a son the nobles acted. They invited the Protestant William of Orange and his wife Mary to come to England as a sort of President, the kind of office he

207

held in Holland with considerable success. He was attracted by the offer because it meant England and Holland would be able to make common cause against Louis XIV's all-powerful France. However he refused to accept unless he was made king and his wife Mary (who was James's daughter) queen. This the nobles conceded, subject to strict limitation of his powers. He landed in the West Country and proceeded towards London. James had a large army stationed on Salisbury Plain blocking the way to London, but at the last minute he refused to lead it and returned to the capital. His army faded away and William advanced unopposed to take over the country. He even helped the incompetent James to escape to France where he stayed for the rest of his life, his only claim to fame being that he was the last English king to rule by divine right which gave him absolute power. The limitations imposed on William by the nobles meant that the King could no longer impose taxes, raise an army or enter into foreign wars without the approval of what became Parliament. So the power of the monarchy began to ebb away and passed to an elected Parliament. As the political franchise was extended, the more democratic the political system became and governments became more and more secular. As a result, the influence of the Church on English politics became weaker and weaker. By the late nineteenth century England was a secular state and the role of the Church was greatly diminished, although even then religion still had enough influence to cause Charles Darwin to hesitate

208

for nearly forty years before publishing his earth-shattering *Origins of the Species*. When he did he started a firestorm among the true believers which continues in some areas to this day.

Whilst England was still ruled by a king who held considerable powers, even if he did not rule by divine right, there were those who were thoroughly dissatisfied with the behaviour of the Church of England and the moral standards of the day. So much so that a group decided to leave England and practise their beliefs in the New World. They were called the Puritans, and they introduced to the New World religious standards similar to Cromwell's. They thrived for a while in what is now the northern New England states but reaction to their strict code set in. Disagreements resulted and people moved away to form many of the Protestant sects that thrive in the United States today. They also unwittingly influenced the American Constitution. The authors of that document made sure that no one person or group could ever achieve total power as enjoyed by the Kings of England who had reigned by divine right. This was achieved by incorporating the famous series of checks and balances. What is less heralded is that they also incorporated wording that ensured that religion was excluded from government, conscious of how it had bedevilled European politics.

Having studied the Christian religion to a limited extent, I then read what I could about Judaism and the Moslem faith. My examinations were cursory but from them I had the following impressions. The history of the Jewish faith did not reveal the complex problems found in Christianity. The only major disagreement appears to be between those Orthodox Jews, who insist on the strict interpretation of the Bible and adherence to its rituals, and the Reform Jews who take a more pragmatic approach to religion. The Moslem world, on the other hand, seems to be going through many of the gyrations of the Christian one, but doing it about a couple of hundred years later. Nevertheless there is no doubt that the Moslem code of behaviour has a lot of similarities with that of both the Christian and Jewish faiths. For the later two religions it is laid down in the Ten Commandments and, whilst those Commandments as such do not appear in the Koran, similar instructions are to be found in it, although in the Moslem Holy Book they are spread throughout the text and not confined to one concise edict as in the Bible.

As a result of my efforts I can view religion as something created by man to bring a civilizing influence to his affairs, and to establish a moral code of behaviour. To a certain extent it also assumed the role now played by today's public health authorities. All these are admirable goals and the world has greatly benefited from the efforts of all those devoted members of all three religions who have over time spread their beliefs. Unfortunately, being created by man, religion contains some of the human weaknesses. As I have described above the lure of power was too great for some of the religious leaders to resist and in pursuit of that power they began to ignore the moral principles they were advocating.

For example, whilst the scriptures told the faithful to love one another they did the other thing: they went

210

to war with one another. They preached that everything and everyone on earth was God's creation and are to be cherished as such. When it came to sexual deviants, however, they conveniently forgot their own instructions and condemned such people to a sort of limbo that still exists in parts of the world today. Worse still the Church of England and the Episcopalian Church in the USA are in danger of splitting apart over this very issue at the beginning of the twenty-first century! What has happened to compassion and charity? I remember my mother telling me that when she went to kindergarten school in England in 1895 children who attempted to write or draw with their left hand were wrapped over the knuckles with a ruler. It was thought at the time that left-handedness was an abnormality not acceptable to God and must be eliminated. However, when the demand for troops during the First World War exceeded supply, anyone left or right handed was accepted into the Army. The left-handers proved that they were just as good riflemen and cannon fodder as their right-handed comrades. So much so that after the war the left-handed stigma was quietly dropped and those who were left handed were absorbed into society as normal human beings. It seems to me that the situation of homosexuals and lesbians is similar to that of the left-handers at the end of the nineteenth century. They are the way they are because they are made that way and there is nothing they can do about that. They are just as much a part of the human race as the rest of us and deserve to be treated as such The fact that some of the leaders of one of the world's major denominations is threatening to break away from the main body over the issue reflects poorly on the Church. It reinforces the view that the Church's conservatism is and always has been a drag on human development. It is no accident that scientific research and industrial advancement flourished earlier in secular states like England and parts of Germany, than in those still under religious control.

The Church's ability to retard development is amply demonstrated in its attitude towards women. All three major religions regard or regarded the female as inferior to the male. She is termed man's handmaiden and until the early part of the twentieth century, even in the Western world, had the same legal status as a house or piece of furniture. She was a man's possession like any other chattel. The churches did not want women to be educated. Their role was to produce children and attend to their husband's needs. So over the last 2,000 years, with a few notable exceptions, no woman has made her mark on history. Is that because none had the ability to do so or was it because they were never allowed to?

I have a friend who is an actuary and he tells me that statistically in every 10 million births there is born one brain with genius or near-genius ability. And the chance of it being in a male or female body is exactly fifty-fifty. I have no idea how such figures are determined or whether they are widely accepted, but the second part of the statement certainly holds true for all of us endowed with somewhat lower intellectual prowess. The females are just as bright as the males. This means that thanks to the religious doctrines of the past two

212

millennia mankind has been deprived of half the services of its most intelligent constituents. Think how much further civilization might have advanced had there been multitudes of Madam Curies, Florence Nightingales and Eleanor Roosevelts. For their part in this tragedy, for tragedy it is, I think the case could be made for claiming that all religions are collectively guilty of the greatest ever crime against humanity.

Thus all my research into the nature of religion leaves me in a somewhat ambivalent state. I admire the civilizing influence it has had on mankind and the charitable work of its members. Because of the way I was programmed in my youth I am still attracted to some of its special services such as those at Easter and the Christmas watch night service, especially if they are conducted in one of the great cathedrals. I still enjoy some of religion's finer music, but of religion itself I am disillusioned. Whilst it has done much good it has also been very divisive and failed to live up to its own moral principles. On balance it has probably retarded rather than advanced man's progress, although on the other hand had it not existed doubtless some other type of authority would have arisen.

I still have complete Faith — my wartime experiences ensured that. So in this mixed-up frame of mind all I can do is live my life to the standards of the Ten Commandments and hope that that will suffice. I also hope that what I have written satisfactorily answers the question as to why I do not attend church regularly, even if it does leave the reader wondering what is the right thing to do. That, like so many other of life's decisions, is one that only he or she can make.

Postscript

Soon after that extraordinary visit to Salisbury cathedral in 1947 I decided that industry and commerce offered better opportunities for a satisfying career than did the Civil Service, so I applied for a number of posts and eventually landed one in the City of London. I learned later that I had been second choice for the job, but as the first choice turned it down when he was offered it I was given the chance to take it. Which I did and by so doing doubled my salary. I served my apprentiship in accounting, finance and international taxation during the seven years that I worked in the City. At the beginning it was hard going, made somewhat more difficult than necessary by the General Manager in the firm who insisted on personally signing all outgoing correspondence. He was a stickler for clear, unambiguous statements written in precise, grammatically correct English. If your letter contained the slightest grammatical imperfection or a possible ambiguity he would send it back to be rewritten. Everybody complained of his dictatorial manner. On the other hand he was a generous employer and often would spend a lot of time explaining to me just why he did not agree with what I had written. He was a very fine accountant and a taxation expert, and would take me with him to visit counsel when we were engaged on an important case. There is no doubt that he was an excellent tutor and I owe him much, for it was he who gave me the confidence and the ability to take on bigger responsibilities later in my career. He was also the one who paid me certainly the greatest if not the only accolade I ever received during my professional life. I had been with the firm for some four years when on one occasion I sent down three letters for signature. Shortly after I had sent them down his secretary phoned to say he wanted to see me. Fearing the worse I made my way down to his office. His secretary warned me that he was not in a very good mood so I gritted my teeth, knocked on his door and went in. He looked up and when he saw who it was grabbed my three letters and threw them at me. In an angry voice he said, "Why do I have to sign all your letters? You know far more about this than I do. In future kindly sign your own letters and take full responsibility for them." As no one else other than directors had that authority that was praise indeed.

By the time my wife and I had lived in the London suburbs for seven years, and both our daughters were born, we began to feel that we would like to escape from London's brick and mortar jungle and return to a more pastoral environment. I also felt that the job I was doing had become repetitious for I could tell what month it was by the particular job I was doing, and although I was well paid I could see no path for advancement. We were, I suppose, both country lovers and felt that London's sprawling suburbia was not an ideal place to raise children. So I started looking for a new job, but the demand for people in the financial field outside London was very limited. I was offered a job in Medan, in what was then called the Dutch East Indies (today's Indonesia), but I did not think that was a very good place to raise children either. Then I was invited to an interview for a job in the East Midlands, wherever that might have been (to most Londoners the world ended at Luton; anything north of that was in the land of the barbarians). I was interviewed not by the company that was seeking a suitable employee but by two partners in the firm's independent auditors. It was not a particularly probing interview and I had no difficulty in answering all their questions. The odd thing about it, though, was that they refused to tell me who they were acting for. They thanked me for attending and said they would be in touch when a final selection was made. I heard nothing from them for over two months and assumed the job had been filled when suddenly I was called to a second interview with the same two audit partners. The only question they asked me this time was whether I was a teetotaller and when I replied that I wasn't, one of them said, "That's all right then; we just thought we should warn you." This time they told me the employer's name and sent me off to an interview with the warning, "If they like the look of your jib, we think they will offer you the job on the spot." Which was just what they did do and I promised to give a decision within seven days. That seven days covered Christmas week and my wife and I spent a long time discussing the pros and cons of the opportunity before us. Should we leave the security of the City position in which I was well established or take a chance on a new life outside of London? In the end we decided that the job met our spec and that I should accept it. It was a decision we have never regretted.

I had to give my City employer two months' notice and when I told the General Manager of my intention he invited me to have lunch with him, not in the canteen but at his club. There he surprised me by saying "You're doing the right thing." He told me that before the war he had been a partner in a small accountancy practice in a county town. He had left it to join our current employer by the lure of a much higher income, and the possibility of advancement. "These things did come about," he said, "except advancement to director level as there is too much nepotism here for that. So for the last thirty years I have run the City rat race when life in that county town would have been so much more relaxed and enjoyable, and I am sorry I ever left it. I shall miss you but for your sake I am glad you are going and I am certain you will do well."

So I left the very formal, professional atmosphere of the City, where surnames only were the order of the day, for the informal, relaxed environment that prevailed in a state-of-the-art engineering company where you were addressed by your Christian name, or by some complex identification which you were given that theoretically showed where you came in a particular hierarchy. It was a cultural shock in more ways than one. Furthermore, that habit of being second

217

choice raised its ugly head again. On the day I reported for work I discovered that I was the second person to hold the post during the last two months. My predecessor, who had come from the firm's auditors, had only been on board for eleven days when the police arrived and arrested him for murdering his girlfriend!

It also came as a bit of a shock to discover that all the Company's senior financial staff from the Financial Director downward were Scots, and that we were collectively referred to by the Lords of Engineering as the "bean counters". As the only Sassenach around my leg was pulled unmercifully by my Scottish colleagues but occasionally I was able to get a shot in of my own. Such as one day when the Olympic Games were taking place and England had qualified for a place in the hockey semi-finals. We, being the accounting/finance staff, were all sat around a table in the canteen one lunchtime (in those days we were not thought worthy of sharing tables with the engineering staff) when I ventured to say that I thought that England was doing very well. Whereupon the Company Secretary promptly declared that hockey was a cissy game; in Scotland they played a real man's game called Hooley. To which I retorted that I was not surprised for obviously the Scots needed something to replace tribal warfare. After that they were a little more careful about commenting on the English. They did, however, concentrate on teaching me most of my bad habits. Through them I learned to appreciate single malt whisky, to put salt instead of sugar on my porridge and to become a rugby fan. They took me up to Murrayfield to watch the international matches and taught me how to eat haggis (you pour neat whiskey over it, shut your eyes and quickly pop it in your mouth). They even tried to turn me into a golfer, but in that they failed for I was too impatient and found the game frustrating. I realized it was good exercise to walk around a golf course but I thought it would be much more beneficial to do so at a brisk pace rather than dawdle around trying to put a little white ball down rabbit holes on the way. This view was confirmed by my cardiologist when in 1966 I had my first heart attack. I was hospitalized for two weeks and kept home for a month before being allowed back to work. I was instructed to take things easy and avoid physical exercise. This I did with the result that in six months I had put on 14lb. So I asked the quack, sorry, doctor, whether there was any form of exercise I could do. He said, "You do not play golf, do you?" When I said no but I was willing to learn, he said, "That is the last thing I want you to do; nobody knows for sure what triggers heart attacks but most cardiologists now consider that stress is a factor. By playing golf you are just replacing one form of stress with another. If you had been a golfer I would have said you can play nine holes if you solemnly promise that the moment you are frustrated you will walk off the course and buy yourself a drink. What I want you to do is take up fishing." When I said that I did not fancy sitting on a river bank watching a float he told me that was not what he had in mind, he wanted me to go fly fishing. He claimed that fly fishing demanded a little manual dexterity which could be acquired in ten minutes, and just enough and only just enough concentration to prevent you worrying about what you had not done today or what you had to do tomorrow. He said you will see many things that you had not noticed before, you will get some exercise for you have to move about, and most importantly, it will allow your mind to relax. Whether you catch fish or not is beside the point. If you do that is an added bonus. As far as relaxing and seeing things is concerned he was proved absolutely correct and I am deeply indebted to him for his advice. I took up fly fishing with the help of my Scottish friends, who claim quite incorrectly that when I eventually caught my first trout I was so exited that I ran up the river bank pulling the wretched fish after me. However, fly fishing did became one of my greatest interests and even now, once a year, I go into the Canadian wilderness in search of the elusive salmon.

By the mid 1990s the company was extending its international interests and I became involved in setting up subsidiary companies in the USA, Canada, France, Brazil, India and a branch office of an English subsidiary in Japan (at that time foreign concerns were not allowed to form Japanese companies). The first time I went back to Japan in the 1960s, the war had been over for nearly twenty years but I was still apprehensive and mentally pictured all the people I had to deal with in military uniform. The situation was not helped by the fact that Tokyo, where we were endeavouring to establish an office, was still in the process of rebuilding. Street lighting was poor and a melancholy atmosphere pervaded the city. Every time I went back, however, there was a marked improvement and my wartime experience to a certain extent prepared me for my dealings with the Japanese. I was involved in negotiations with a number of companies and the pattern was always the same. You would find yourself sitting on one side of a long table with your interpreter by your side. On the other side of the table and directly opposite you would be the senior Japanese executive. Some six or eight assistants would be sat on each side of him. He would be the only one to speak to you but in between his remarks to you, whispered conversations would flow up and down the ranks of assistants. This resulted in very slow progress which frustrated many occidentals. To me it seemed if not normal then at least understandable. I knew what they were doing. What I termed assistants were in fact executives involved in the project being negotiated. They all had had their say on how to proceed in the negotiation and what they hoped to achieve. Now they were there to give advice to their leader as the negotiation progressed. In this way they would all know of all the problems encountered during the negotiations and in the time-honoured Japanese tradition be collectively responsible for the end result. Just as in their engineering departments a drawing by any engineer had to be passed up the chain of his superiors for their chop of approval before it was accepted, thus ensuring collective responsibility and useful training for junior engineers. One thing I liked about negotiating with the Japanese was that in my experience, once a clause was agreed or a number settled that was it, they never went back to it and tried to reopen the issue. That was not always the case in negotiations with the Americans. There were always numerous lawyers involved on both sides in such negotiations. They did most of the talking and from time to time would play what I called the third-man technique. It usually happened when one side needed time to think or upset the other side's train of thought. At that point the third man would jump in and ask some totally unrelated question, or raise a point about something that had been settled earlier. He would try to reopen the matter and although his interruption might not last for long it gave his colleagues the breathing space they required (our lawyers did not call these chaps third men — they referred to them as professional horses asses).

During my business visits to Japan I never disclosed that I had once been a POW there, but I was caught out when in 1969 I accompanied the Chairman and the Marketing Director on a visit to Japan. By that time the transformation of Tokyo into today's brightly lit city was complete and I felt quite at home there. Arrangements had been made by our local manager for visits to be made to four important Japanese companies and each visit was scheduled for 10.00 a.m. on four consecutive days. In accordance with Japanese custom that meant that we had to arrive at the door of the Japanese establishment at exactly ten o'clock. There Japanese officers of the host company of the same rank as the visiting officials would be waiting to welcome us. Our local manager timed our arrival to the first of our visits to the second. We stepped out of our car at exactly

10.00 a.m. and there on the steps of the Japanese company's office stood the company's Chairman, Marketing Director and Commercial Director. Our Chairman, who had never been to Japan before, stepped forward to shake hands with the Chairman of the Japanese company. That gentleman hesitated and for a moment did not seem to know what to do. One of the interpreters spoke quietly to him and he somewhat hesitatingly shook our Chairman's hand. He did the same with our Marketing Director but when it came to my turn, without thinking I did not hold my hand out, instinctively I bowed the correct bow for someone of senior rank. He returned the bow and from that moment I was a marked man. During that visit and at the other three factories we visited there were always two Japanese at my side. I think they thought that I could both speak and read their language. They were quite wrong, of course — I only knew the numbers and a few words that are not spoken in polite society.

Whilst I was in Tokyo on that occasion my history inevitably became known to the British Embassy officials. They asked me the question I am still asked even today: "What do you think of the Japanese?" I do not find it an easy question to answer. Had it been put to me sixty years ago it would have been easy and I would have said I hate them. Now I am not so sure. I understand and can now appreciate that the Japanese soldiers were not just being patriotic as we were but were conforming to a code of honour (reinforced by a little propaganda) which demanded total sacrifice for the Emperor. They were told by their fathers not to disgrace the family honour. Live to the standard of the warrior code and if necessary give your life for the Emperor; never surrender. And of course they never did, and one has to respect their bravery. I do not condone their inhuman behaviour but I no longer hate all of them as once I did. The exceptions include the first commander of Hong Kong for his treatment of the civilian population of the Colony, and his refusal to permit life-saving diphtheria serum to be brought into Sham Shui Po camp when there was an epidemic of the disease there. Another exception is the Narumi Camp Commandant (aka the Bastard) and his gang of thugs for mistreatment of prisoners in general, and their obvious enjoyment in torturing downed US airmen.

Not long after the bowing incident there arose the need for someone to manage all our North American affairs and I was offered the post. So once again my wife and I were faced with a difficult decision. We were happy where we were and at fifty-five did we really want to start a new life in a strange land? Not that it was particularly strange to me for I had visited many times, but visiting a foreign country and staying in a hotel, and living in that country are two different things. My wife thought that it would give us a new lease on life and I remembered the American General on the USS *Admiral Hughes*. That larger-than-life American character, who in defiance of all the accounting regulations, had paid one thousand British ex-POWs US$20 each when we were crossing the Pacific on our way home after the war. We decided to accept the offer and are very glad we did.

The initial contract was for four years but I stayed for ten and then went back for four years as a consultant. So I was seventy when I finally retired and by that time it was too late to return to England. We were established in America and liked it. The climate suited us fine and we did not suffer from the catarrh which always plagued us in England each winter. One daughter was married to an American and the other was leading the nomadic life of a wife of a British Army officer, so the decision to stay was not difficult. Retirement should have given us time for some leisurely travel but my mother-in-law was widowed and suffered from advanced Alzheimer's disease. We therefore managed to get her over to live with us and over the next ten years that made travel very difficult. It did mean, though, that I had time to research some of the things I wrote about in the last chapter and to make three visits on my own to my favourite city, Hong Kong, which is in many ways my alma mater.

I had passed through Hong Kong on a few business trips before my retirement in 1985 and so had some idea of its fantastic growth since the war. I was never there long enough, though, to look for the graves of my comrades who had died there. I did manage to find the site of the Sham Shui Po camp, which had been completely built over and the only thing I recognized was the Jubilee Terrace building on the waterfront. It was occupied by Chinese families and I did not attempt to go in. However, it was not until I made lengthy stays there in 1997 and 1998 that I realized the magnitude of Hong Kong's accomplishment. It was also during these stays that I found the graves of fallen shipmates. They were not in the main military cemetery but in a small one half a mile from Stanley market and some 12 miles from the principal town, Victoria. I recognized six of the names on the gravestones including those of Warrant Officer Yeoman Mitchell and Coder Percy Cook. Percy was one of the last "hostilities only" chaps to be sent to the Colony and the first to die in the prison camps. He was the lad I saw being taken away on a stretcher from the unsavoury North Point camp with flies on his face. Standing there by his grave brought back so many memories of the world of my youth and I wondered once again what factors lead to me standing there when I might well have been lying next to him.

As for Hong Kong's accomplishments, the physical changes are impressive: there are tunnels under the harbour and through the hills, expressways where once there were only tracks, a superb international airport, a first-class subway system, a skyline in Victoria that rivals New York's and the once sleazy Wanchai is now the high-rent district! Two whole cities with populations greater than Philadelphia in the US or Birmingham in England have sprung up in the New Territories, where once there were only duck farms. The sleepy little village at Aberdeen, where the auxiliary naval dockyard was situated, is now a forest of high-rise apartments and home to fancy floating restaurants. Whereas Lane Crawford was the only European-type department store in my day, all the regulars of Bond Street and Fifth Avenue have now set up stall both in Victoria and in the extensive Kowloon shopping malls. The principal Naval Dockyard in Victoria, with its large graving dock and workshops, has disappeared under a layer of asphalt. Stonecutters Island, with its tall radio masts through which we communicated with the Admiralty in London every night, is an island no more. It, like the dockyard, has been sacrificed on the altar of land reclamation. The Peak tram still operates but the bungalow on the Peak in which once I lived is no more. The whole topography of the area adjacent to the upper terminus of the tram has changed, although not in my opinion for the better. So whilst I found no physical evidence of the buildings where once I lived and worked, I did find something that I well remembered from my Navy days. On a whim I took a ferry to Lantau Island and a bus up to the Buddhist monastery. There, unchanged and unchanging, the Great Golden Buddha sat serenely on his hilltop. This time I did not attempt to climb all the steps to the base of the huge statue. As before, though, I wondered how it was built. What was underneath that golden skin that enabled it to sit on its hilltop and defy everything nature could throw at it? Which included typhoons with wind speeds of over a hundred miles an hour.

Although the Great Buddha had not changed there were changes in the monastery courtyard. The joss sticks were still there but few stalls sold prayer cards, prayer wheels or religious texts. Instead most of them now sold CDs, some of which were being played through loudspeakers stationed around the courtyard. It was mostly chants that were being played and some were very good, so I bought a couple and still play them from time to time. In the monastery's entrance hall the three brightly dressed, huge, standing Buddha statues were still there in their glass cases. The familiar aroma of burning incense filled the air as it had done in 1941. The atmosphere within the monastery was much as I remembered it. Like most major religious establishments it inspired respect and one tended to speak in hushed tones. It was a different story just outside the monastery walls. Cafés and souvenir stalls abounded, whereas none were there when first I visited. In front of one café I saw a small Chinese boy dressed in traditional style. His bright-red outfit caught my eye and I took his picture. His mother, dressed in a very smart European-style business suit came out to collect him. I said, "I hope you do not mind me taking the boy's photograph."

"Not at all," she said in perfect English and asked me where I came from. When I told her Connecticut, USA, she said, "Oh, we are near neighbors. We live in Brooklyn, New York where my son was born. We are here to visit my parents. Would you care to come and meet them?"

So I did and learned a lot about present-day conditions in the ex-colony. As far as my informants were concerned their lives had not changed in the slightest since Hong Kong became part of China. I also realized that the picture I had taken was not of a Chinese boy at all: I had taken one of an American boy. No wonder his mother was smiling — the world really has moved on since 1941.

Striking as these physical changes are from the Hong Kong of the 1940s, what impressed me even more are things that are missing from the present-day scene. To me the harbour, that tract of water between Victoria and Kowloon, seems strangely empty. Except for a large gambling vessel moored in Kowloon docks in roughly the same place as the old *Elenga* docked in 1940, the only activity taking place seems to be confined to a few ferries and pleasure craft, with the odd dredger lumbering through. In my day it had been crowded with merchant ships secured to buoys scattered throughout the harbour. Weaving between them were innumerable sampans and junks, whilst lighters were secured alongside. Into these, cargoes were unloaded and from them fresh cargoes were hauled aboard, the work being done partly with the use of the ships gantries and partly by hordes of coolies. President Lines liners from the United States docked regularly in Kowloon (bringing mail from the UK) and our destroyers and river gunboats moved cautiously through the teeming traffic. Now all that hive of activity has left the harbour. The warships and liners have departed, the latter driven out of business by the aeroplane. The merchant ships have also gone — they could not survive in a world that makes a god of productivity. Their replacements are super-efficient container ships whose diesel engines propel them across the world's oceans at speeds in excess of 20 knots and whose skeleton crews have more in common with computer wizards than the master mariners of my day. Such ships do not function in crowded harbours as did the tramp steamers and merchantmen of the 1940s. Not for them the indignity of being loaded or unloaded by human hand or being forced to use onboard equipment to do the job. They demand and have been given special ports of their own called container terminals. One such now covers some 2 miles of Kowloon's western shore from just north of the site of the Sham Shui Po prison camp all the way to Kwai Chung.

Another victim of technological progress is the rickshaw. They were everywhere before the war and for many the preferred mode of transport. I could never bring myself to use one — it seemed to me that there was something intrinsically wrong about a man having to demean himself by pulling another perfectly fit human being around in order to earn a living. I suppose it is an illogical quirk of mine because I feel the same way about having my shoes polished by the shoeshine merchants outside Grand Central Station in New York. In any event, the rickshaw is now to me conspicuous by its absence, its place having been taken by a fleet of ubiquitous dark-red Toyota taxis.

However the one thing missing from the current scene that most impresses me has nothing to do with technology — it is the absence of a multitude of homeless people. In 1941 the population of Hong Kong was estimated at 2½ million of which approximately one tenth were thought to be homeless. They lived on the streets and slept all along the side walks from Wanchai to Causeway Bay. Now, despite having absorbed waves of refugees and with its

230

population increased to some 6½ million, this symptom of extreme poverty is not apparent in the city. In fact, the per capita income in Hong Kong now exceeds that in England and Canada. It is a very impressive transformation and reflects great credit on all who helped bring it about. First and foremost of these must be the industrious, hard-working inhabitants themselves and their entrepreneurial expertise. The influx of capital from overseas and the technical skills it brought with it also played an important role as did the Colony's emergence as the major financial centre in the South-East Pacific region. Considerable credit must go to the Colony's government for it set the stage for the territory's economic development. It provided what was scarce on the Pacific Rim, incorruptible administration, financial transparency, freedom of the press and respect for the individual. Couple this with a stable currency, a sophisticated, well-established legal system, a respected judiciary and an efficient police force and it is easy to understand why Hong Kong attracted both investors and refugees. It may not have been as democratic a government as some would wish but to the extent that it was dictatorial it was a benign dictatorship. The colonial power, itself one of the world's great democracies, ensured that it stayed that way. Thus the Colony enjoyed what is probably the best and certainly the most efficient form of government. Its staff of professional administrators had no need to spend time and effort raising election funds. Not for them the obsession with opinion polls or the tyranny of powerful lobbies. They had no requirement for personal publicity and were able to devote all their time and energy to the pursuit of good government. Judging by the speed that most Western democracies get things done, Hong Kong was fortunate to have such a professional administration. It is difficult to imagine a fully democratic government approving, financing and executing all the major engineering projects that have been completed in Hong Kong since the war. It would have spent too much time debating and arguing about them, and trying to reconcile all the diverse requirements of self-interested pressure groups.

In any event, the city has now returned to China but to a large extent appears to be self-governing. It is well equipped to do so for Chinese nationals have long since moved into the top government administrative posts and at the time of the handover the head of the Civil Service was a Chinese lady. It seems probable therefore that the principles and standards that developed Hong Kong from a fever-ridden, pirate haven to the richest mega metropolis between Tokyo and Singapore will not readily be forgotten and I wish it well.

Appendix

Ships Sunk in the Pacific Area Whilst Carrying Allied POWs

Montevideo Maru 1 July 1942, torpedoed off Bagador Lighthouse east of Luzon. POWs embarked 1,053. Survivors none.

Kachidoki Maru 12 September 1942, torpedoed off East Hainan Island. POWs embarked 950. Survivors 515.

Lisbon Maru 2 October 1942, torpedoed near Tung Fusham Island, China Sea. POWs embarked 1,816. Survivors 977.

Nichimei Maru 15 January 1943, torpedoed between Singapore and Moulmein. POWs embarked 1,000. Survivors 947.

Suez Maru 29 September 1943, torpedoed off Kangean Island. POWs embarked 548. Survivors none.

Tamabuko Maru 24 June 1944, torpedoed off Goto Nagasaki. POWs embarked 772. Survivors 212.

Haragiku Maru	26 June 1944, torpedoed off Belawan. POWs embarked 720. Survivors 543.
Rakuyo Maru	12 September 1944, torpedoed off East Hainan Island. POWs embarked 1,214. Survivors 135.
Shinyu Maru	17 September 1944, off Mindanao. POWs embarked 750. Survivors none.
Junyo Maru	19 September 1944, torpedoed en route Java/Japan. POWs embarked 2,200. Survivors 723.
Toyofuku Maru	21 September 1944, north-west of Philippine Islands. POWs embarked 1,287. Survivors 380.
Arisan Maru	24 October 1944, torpedoed Bashi Straits. POWs embarked 1,782. Survivors none.
Oryoku Maru *Enoura Maru* *Brazil Maru*	9 January 1945, all three ships sunk by Allied aircraft in Bay of Takaa. POWs embarked 1,620. Survivors 618.